D1615051

LET'S GARDEN

LET'S GARDEN

Enid Blyton

Illustrated by
William McLaren

Purnell
Greater London House
London NW1

A PURNELL BOOK

© Darrell Waters Limited, 1948
Enid Blyton is the trademark of Darrell Waters Ltd.

First published in Great Britain in 1948 by
Latimer House Limited
33 Ludgate Hill
London EC4

This edition published in 1987 by
Macdonald & Company (Publishers) Ltd
London & Sydney
A BPCC plc company

Typeset by Goodfellow & Egan, Cambridge
Printed and bound in Great Britain
by A. J. Acford

Macdonald & Company (Publishers) Ltd
Greater London House
Hampstead Road
London NW1 7QX

Consultant and text editor for revised edition: Susan Conder
Front cover artwork: Cynthia Pow
Editor: Clare Dannatt
Designer: Sarah Williams
Production: Ken Holt

British Library Cataloguing in Publication Data
Blyton, Enid
Let's garden.
1. Gardening
I. Title
635   SB450.97

ISBN 0-361-07550-2

CONTENTS

CHAPTER I

YOUR GARDEN TOOLS

So you are going to have a garden. Well, you could not play a nicer game or do more interesting work than gardening. You will make things grow, you will cut the flowers that blossom in your garden, and you will eat the vegetables and salads that sprout so willingly under your busy hands. What fun!

Do you know much about gardening? Have you had a garden before? I wonder! It is an interesting, all-the-year-round job, for there is always something to do in each of the twelve months. It is just as much fun to dig up old plants and have a bonfire in November as it is to go and cut a bunch of roses for your dining table in June. You will have a much better garden in the summer-time if you work in it during the winter months. So we will be all-the-year-round gardeners—don't you think so?

It is cold and often wet in the garden during the winter, and you may get dirty and damp. So make sure you have an old coat, a short warm scarf, and good strong boots to go gardening in when the bad weather is here. Then it doesn't matter how dirty you get, your gardening clothes will stand it, and you will be happy because you can do exactly what you like in them.

To garden properly you must have tools. You need not have many, but you must have the right sort. If I were going to buy some for you, these are what I should get:

Spade—Strong, and the right size for you. It is no use having a kind of seaside spade. You must have a proper garden spade, not too heavy for you, nor too big. You will have digging to do, and a good spade will make it easy.

Fork—You will need this for forking over the ground, and for forking up weeds to burn or bury them. It should be a strong one and your size.

Rake—You will find this useful in raking off stones and in breaking up the surface soil to get it smooth and even. Get one your size if you can.

Dutch hoe—There are two kinds of hoe, the flat kind which is the Dutch hoe, and the bent hoe, called the draw hoe. You can do without the draw hoe, if necessary, but the Dutch hoe is very helpful. You will be able to use it every day in the summer-time to loosen the earth around your plants, so that air may get into the soil, moisture will not escape so much, and surface weeds will be destroyed. You may not be able to get a Dutch hoe your size, but if not, you can get the handle shortened for yourself, and use it easily that way. There is an improved type of Dutch hoe, too, called a "Swoe" or "Saynor". Many people find this the most useful type of all.

Trowel—A strong one for planting or for lifting plants.

Small hand fork—This is useful for many things.

Hand-line—You must be able to plant your seeds in even rows, especially when growing vegetables, and to do this you need a length of stout string which you can stretch over your garden to give you a straight line. You can make your own hand-line. Find two pieces of strong stick and tie a stout piece of string or a few yards of thin cord to them—one end to each stick. There is your hand-line all ready for you!

Wheelbarrow—I expect you already have one you can use. It should be strong enough and big enough to do all the work you want it for, and light enough not to tire you too much. That is the kind I should buy for you if I were choosing your garden tools.

9

Watering can—This should not be too large or it will be heavy when filled with water. A strong one is best, with two roses for the spout—one a fine-holed rose, the other a coarse-holed rose.

Hose—You will find a hose useful if your parents have one, especially if your garden is a big one.

Secateurs—Double-cut or "parrot-beak" secateurs are best. They are very sharp, so be careful when you use them to cut flowers and harvest vegetables from your garden.

Dibber—A wooden or stainless steel dibber will help you make holes in the ground or in compost in seed trays for planting seedlings. Many people use a pencil, and that is fine, too.

These are all the tools you will need. You must remember always to put them away bright and clean. You may know good workers by their tools. Bright, shining tools always belong to those who do their work well, take a pride in it, and enjoy it. Dull and dirty tools belong to the slackers.

Rub your tools well after you have used them and see that they are clean and dry when you put them away. If you put them away wet, they may rust and become blunt. Never leave them out in the garden. Have a special place for them in a shed, if you can, so that you always know where they are and don't need to waste half your time hunting for them before you begin gardening.

You may have to wait for a birthday or for Christmas before you get your tools, but never mind, make do with what you have till then. Once the grown-ups see that you really *are* keen about gardening they will be pleased to give you the tools you want. You can easily tell them about all the tools in this chapter.

Just one more thing before this chapter ends—if you haven't done very much gardening before, go slowly at first, or you will have all sorts of stiffnesses! If you go out suddenly and dig all day long, you won't want to do any digging at all the next day, which would be a pity. Go slowly until you are used to gardening, and then you can do anything you like, and will soon be as strong as a horse.

CHAPTER II

PREPARING YOUR GARDEN

WHERE IS your garden, I wonder? In the valley where you get plenty of warmth and good soil? On the stony hillside? Does it face north or south? I don't know, so I shall have to hope that it is at any rate as nice a piece as you can get. Some grown-ups give their children a piece of ground that is hidden away in a shrubbery somewhere, or some other piece that is really not of much use for a garden. This is because they think you will soon be tired of gardening, or will not keep your garden pretty and neat.

So you must explain to your parents that you do seriously want to garden all the year round and mean to make your piece of garden as pretty or as useful as theirs. Therefore you must have a chance to do your best, and a good piece of ground will not be wasted on you. If you tell them this they will believe you, and probably let you have a really nice piece of ground that will grow anything you want. It is most heart-breaking to be given a piece of garden that won't grow anything at all because of overhanging trees, too much cold clay, or something like that, no matter how hard you work or what you do. So do try to have a really nice piece of ground, with good soil, sunshine, and air, and then keep your word and garden properly. You will feel very proud if your parents take their visitors to see your garden, instead of hoping they won't notice it.

Now we will suppose you have chosen the nicest piece of ground possible for you, well out in the sunshine, and with good soil. If your garden is an old one, I expect the soil will be just right for you, and will grow anything. But if the garden is new, things will not be quite so easy.

Look at your soil. Is is clayey? Does it get as hard as a brick in the summer, and in the winter is it wet and sticky? If so, then you have clay in it.

Perhaps your soil is very stony, and always seems dry in the summer-time. If so, you have gravel soil.

If your soil is clayey, you must dig it well in the autumn, and leave it in big lumps for the frost to get into. It will break up the clods and make them powdery for you. Whenever you have a bonfire, save the ashes and dig them into the clay soil. That will help a good deal.

For sandy or stony soil you may save your decayed leaves and weeds. Put the leaves, except for holly and plane tree leaves, which are very slow to rot, in a big pile. When the leaves have rotted, you can use the leaf mould to improve your soil. Weeds should go on a compost heap, together with vegetable peel from the kitchen and grass cuttings. They will rot down, too, into rich, dark compost. Dig the leaf mould or compost well into your garden and it will help to nourish the soil, which will keep its moisture better. Decaying weeds or vegetable matter are also called *humus*, and it is always a good thing to fork humus into any ground during the autumn. The plants you grow take a great deal of goodness out of the ground, and the humus we fork in gives back the goodness that the next batch of plants will need.

I hope your soil is a mixture of sand, humus, and clay, for this is the best kind for a garden. It is called *loam*, and we shall certainly be able to grow a fine garden if we have a good loam to work in. But even if we have not, we can help to make our soil good and can make a success of our garden.

In the autumn we must dig over our garden well. All gardeners do this. They have pulled up the plants that have died, and have cleared the beds as much as they can. Good digging will prepare the soil for next year. It will enable the air, the sunshine, and the frost to get down into the earth; it will turn up many harmful grubs which the birds will eat for us.

Do you know how to dig your garden? There is a special way. It is a good way, a quick way, and a tidy way, and that is why proper gardeners use it.

You must dig across your garden, beginning from the right. Dig in a straight line, drive your spade straight down, not slanting, turn over each spadeful and throw it in front of you, so that, at the end of the row, you have a straight hill of earth and beside it a trench.

Now, if you have any manure, or humus, for your soil (and I hope you have), you must neatly fork it into your trench, all along the bottom. Now start digging again, this time from the left, just behind your trench, and *throw every spadeful into the trench, covering up the manure as you go.* Now you have another trench and into this you may also fork manure or humus. Then once again start digging from the right, filling up with your spadefuls of earth the second trench, and making a third trench as you go. Go on like this until you have dug the whole of your garden, and have dug out the last trench of all. Where is the earth to fill it? There it is, at the top of the garden—the earth you threw out of the first trench of all and made into a long hill! Fetch it and put it into your last trench.

Digging and manuring in this way is great fun. You will like it. Don't do it all at once if your garden is big. There is plenty of time. It is a lovely feeling when it is all done. You will stand and look at your brown, dug-over garden, knowing that deep inside is the manure or humus doing its good work, and that every bit of your garden has been lifted and changed. Frost will get to it and break it up still further. I am sure you will enjoy your tea on the day that you have finished digging over your garden!

CHAPTER III

WHAT FLOWERS TO GROW THIS SPRING

IT IS most exciting to choose what seeds to plant in springtime. All the garden centres and nurseries are filled with brightly coloured packets of scores of different seeds, and it is difficult to choose which to buy. I will help you to choose them this first year, and then next year you will know enough to go and choose any others you like.

We usually sow seeds of annuals in late March or early April. If you live in the south of Britain, you may sow your seeds in March, but if your home is in the north, then you will usually be wiser to wait until April. Seeds will not grow if the weather is frosty or bitter.

Do you know what annuals are? I expect you all know them as big books that come out once a year at Christmas time! But in the gardening world they are plants that grow, flower, and die all in the same year. They have a one-year life. Some plants have a two-year life, others live for many, many years. These I will tell you about in another chapter. At present I want to tell you all about annuals, because we shall grow mostly those this year.

The best thing for you to do in February is to get a seed catalogue from either a garden centre in your town, or write for one from one of the famous seed firms. A really good catalogue will give you pictures and photographs of the various flowers, and then you can see exactly what they are like before choosing them. You will want to know the prices of the seeds too, because, if you are buying them yourself, you will only have a certain amount of money to spend. Christmas money will come in very useful for buying your seeds, so put some by for that.

When you have your catalogue, look carefully through it. There will be dozens of flowers you have never even heard of. Look for the following flowers, all of which will grow in your garden, whether you live in the town or in the country:

Candytuft, Shirley poppies, marigolds, Virginian stock, nasturtiums, clarkia, mignonette, cornflowers, mallow (usually called *Lavatera* in catalogues), Californian poppies (catalogue name is *Eschscholtzia* —pronounced escolshea), love-in-a-mist (or *Nigella*), sweet peas, and sunflowers. There is a good choice of plants for you here, and all of them will grow easily and well, if you look after them in the right way. Read what the catalogue says about them, and see which flowers you like the best. You cannot grow all of them this year if your garden is small, so choose your favourites.

When you have made up your mind which seeds you want, write our your list and go to buy them. You will probably see a tall stand of seed-packets at the garden centre. Study them whenever you have a chance, for you will soon get to know a great many different flowers by their pictures.

Remember to buy *fresh* seeds. You are going to spend time and trouble on them, and only good things are worth that. Look at the date on the seed packet. If it is last year's date, the seeds might not germinate. When seeds are remaindered, it is often because they are old. Some garden centres have packets of mixed seed of easy-to-grow annuals, especially for children's gardens. These packets are very often good value for money, and will help you fill your garden with colourful flowers.

Look at the seeds you buy. Each kind is different. Do you like the little flat yellow seeds of the candy-tuft? Have you any sunflower seeds? Some of them are beautifully marked. Then look at the funny little brush-seeds of the cornflower, and the tiny black seeds of the poppy. How different they are!

Now you have your seeds and you are waiting for the right day to sow them. Did you dig over your garden in the autumn? Perhaps you didn't have it then, and it wants preparing now. If so, dig it over in February. Look at it again in March. There are sure to be big clods of earth here and there, drying

18

in the March wind. You can break those up. The soil should be nice and damp, ready for the seeds.

The right day for sowing seeds is a warm day, with no frost, no high wind, no pouring rain. If you can, choose an hour or two after a shower, and then the ground will be moist, ready for the seeds. A windy day is no good, because your seeds will be blown away. You want the sort of day on which people say, "Ah, spring is coming at last!"

Go out to your garden. Is the soil smooth and even? Your seeds will put out very tiny roots, only able to deal with fine grains of soil. They cannot tackle big lumps and clods. Break down the clods with your rake, until your soil has a fine, even surface. Does the earth seem too dry? Water it a little, then, before sowing your seeds.

If you are going to sow your seeds in a straight line, you will need your hand-line. Get it and put a stick at one end of the bed. Unroll the cord from the stick and put the other stick where you want it, letting the string run straight over your bed. Now take a sharp stick and run it along the soil under the string. You will get a perfectly straight line then. Are your seeds very small? Then make a very shallow furrow indeed! The smaller the seed, the shallower the drill; the bigger the seed, the deeper. That is easy to remember, isn't it?

Very small seeds, such as poppy, you must plant carefully, or a careless shake of your hand will send half the seeds flying out of the packet far and wide over the soil! That would never do. A good idea is to mix the tiny seeds with sand or a crumbled-up handful of soil. Then you can shake out sand and seeds together into the drill with no fear of planting them too thickly.

Big seeds, such as sunflower or nasturtium, you must plant one by one. You can make little holes for each one about 2.5 centimetres deep and drop them in. Cover up carefully.

If you are growing Virginian stock for an edging to your bed (it makes a lovely one), you can sow that thickly. It has thin, straggling stalks and needs to be grown in a mass. But sow other seeds thinly or you will have a crowd of tiny plants pressed together, and none of them will have enough light or air.

Using your feet or the back of your rake, cover your seeds with a layer of fine soil. Some seeds you will want to grow in patches or rings, not in lines. It is best to draw a ring round them with a stick, after planting, as then you will know exactly where the patch is.

You must put a label in the patch to tell you what seeds are there. You can buy (or borrow from your parents) a few plastic labels. Write the name of your seeds on each one and put it in its right place.

Of course you will not water your seeds immediately after sowing them, or you will swamp them out of the ground. You should not water them until they are showing green through the ground, unless the weather is very dry. If this happens, you should water them from time to time, adjusting your hose nozzle to give a fine spray, or using the fine rose on your watering can.

You will have to wait two or three weeks before your seeds come through. Do not disturb the bed to see if they are growing. They will come through in their own good time. A cold snap will keep them back; a moist, warm spell will hurry them on. It all depends on the weather.

You will be pleased when at last you see them breaking through the soil in green patches and lines. Keep your bed well weeded, for you must not allow robber-plants to steal the space and light you need for your seedlings.

Water when your garden needs it—but probably it will not need much help in that way, unless you have very sandy soil. Remember that the best time to water is at night when the sun is down. Remember to use a watering can with a fine rose on the spout, or the hose nozzle adjusted to give a fine spray, so that the water comes out gently, not in a gush. If you flood your plants they will become loosened at the roots, and that is bad for them.

It is very important to give your plants the right place in your garden—tall ones usually go at the back, small ones at the edges, medium ones in between. Sometimes, though, it looks pretty to have one or two tall plants at the front, just for a change. To set your garden out properly you will need to know how high each plant grows, and so in the next chapter I will tell you about each of the annuals mentioned as seeds in this. Then you can arrange your seeds properly in the bed, and your garden will look well planned instead of slipshod and untidy.

CHAPTER IV

ANNUALS, BIG AND SMALL

I SHALL begin with the tallest annuals and finish with the smallest.

Sunflowers—Sunflowers are of many kinds. Some grow only 90 centimetres tall, some may be as high as 3 metres. You will love the giant sunflowers with their big, friendly faces; but unless your garden is large it is best not to grow the giants, for they are really too big. Save the big heads of seeds when ripe, because the finches in your garden will be very pleased to come and peck them out in the winter-time if you hang them up somewhere. Sunflowers must always be placed at the back of your garden.

Sweet Peas—These, as you know, are climbing plants, and therefore must also be placed at the back of the garden, and must have sticks to support them. They need special care, and I will tell you more about them later on (Chapter VI), so that you can grow them well. They will climb 1.8–2.1 metres high. There are dwarf forms, too, that do not need staking and are only 30 centimetres high. These are lovely for edging your garden.

Rose Mallow (or *Lavatera*)—This is a pretty plant to grow. It has pink, red or white flowers, and grows about 90 centimetres high. It will look well at the back of your plot.

Clarkia—This is a very lovely and decorative annual. Its rosette-like flowers may be salmon pink, crimson, lilac, pinky-mauve, or pure white. They grow in tall, graceful spires, and are about 75 centimetres high. They will like a middle place in your garden. They are useful for cutting because they last a long time in water.

Cornflowers—You are sure to know these pretty flowers. The plants grow from 45–75 centimetres high, sometimes higher. They will do either at the back of your garden or in the middle. The flowers are a bright blue, a reddish mauve, or white. Blue cornflowers are a great favourite with nearly everybody.

Love-in-a-Mist (or *Nigella*)—This grows about 45 centimetres high and is a charming blue flower, the blossom lost in a misty green haze of finely-cut-up foliage. A very old favourite. There are mixed shades, too, of white, pink, purple, blue and mauve.

Mignonette—This we grow not so much for its appearance, which is rather sober, but for its delicious scent. A few pieces of mignonette in a vase will scent the whole room. The flowers are a dull red-green and grow upwards in a spike. Plant mignonette thickly and it will grow about 25 centimetres high. Plant it thinly and it will make big plants about 45 centimetres high. You must choose what height you want it and plant accordingly.

Pot Marigold (*Calendula*)—This bright orange or yellow flower will grow anywhere and everywhere, in the poorest soil. Its height is about 45 centimetres, and it will give you plenty of blossoms.

Californian Poppy (or *Eschscholtzia*)—I hope you will grow some of these because they are so pretty and bright. The flowers are a brilliant orange-gold, silky and fragile, and the leaves are feathery-looking and blue-green in colour. The poppy-like flowers are colourful all the summer through. You may get mixed colours if you like—white, yellow, pink, and red—or simply have the bright yellow. The flowers have odd little green caps which they push off their heads when the buds open. You may grow it as an edging to your garden, or as separate plants, which-ever you like. It will be quite good as an edging if you don't mind it looking a little untidy later on. It grows about 30 centimetres high.

Candytuft—This is another easily grown and pretty flower. Its height is about 30 centimetres. It has fine heads of flowers—pink, white, and red.

Shirley Poppy—You are sure to know the lovely little Shirley poppy and will like to grow it. The flowers themselves do not last long, but you will have plenty. Like the Californian poppies, they throw off their green, two-sided caps, and then shake out their pretty petals in the sunshine. You must remember to look at their seed-heads when the poppies are over. Each seed-head has a number of little holes in it, and when the wind blows the heads shake and the seeds fly out. The flowers are red, pink, and white, and grow about 30 centimetres high.

Dwarf Nasturtium—This is another plant which does not need good soil or very much care, for it will flourish almost anywhere. It grows 20–22.5 centimetres high. You will like it as an edging, or as separate plants. It has masses of flowers, bright

yellow or orange-red, with long spurs. You are sure
to know its round, flat leaves, quite unlike those of
other flowers.

Virginian Stock—I am sure you will like to grow
this merry little flower as an edging to your bed. Do
you know those sweets called "hundreds and thousands" because they are so very, very small? Well, I
always think that Virginian stock is the "hundreds
and thousands" of the flower world, because it puts
out so many, many tiny flowers—pink, crimson,
white, and lilac, like the real "hundreds and thousands". Plant it thickly. It will grow 17.5–20 centimetres high.

There are a few other annuals you can grow as
climbers, besides sweet peas, but these you will find
in the chapter on climbing plants.

Make your choice of the annuals I have described
to you, and then work out where you will plant
them in your bed. In the next chapter I will give
you a few little garden plans to show you how you
may plant your annuals to best advantage.

Next year you may try such flowers as annual
lupins, annual larkspur, scabious and godetia, or
sweet alyssum (for a border edging). It is best not to
try too many the first year. I think six or eight are
best to begin with.

CHAPTER V

A FEW GARDEN PLANS

Is your garden a round one, a square one, or an oblong one? Perhaps it is an oval, or maybe just a long narrow strip. I will give you plans for each kind. As you will see, it is quite easy to plan your garden properly, because, providing you put the tallest plants at the back and the small ones in the front, you can't very well go wrong. If it is a bed you can walk round, then put the tallest plants in the middle. You can, if you wish, put some tall plants at the front of a bed, providing they don't hide little plants behind. I think perhaps it may help you to see some plans.

The first one is for a square garden. Here it is:

Another plan for a smaller square garden:

A plan for a very little garden:

BACK

CORNFLOWERS	
CANDYTUFT	CLARKIA
VIRGINIAN STOCK	

Two plans for a round garden:

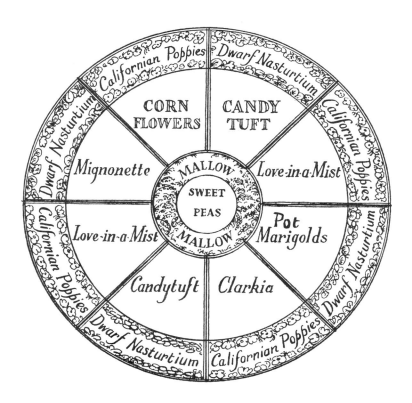

LET'S GARDEN

If your garden is oval, you can adapt the round plans quite easily. Now here is a plan for an oblong garden:

BACK

	GIANT SUNFLOWERS OR CANARY CREEPER	
CLARKIA	CORNFLOWERS / DWARF NASTURTIUM	CANDYTUFT
CALIFORNIAN POPPIES	VIRGINIAN STOCK	CALIFORNIAN POPPIES

Perhaps your garden is merely a long strip between two paths, without a proper back or front. Very well—put your tallest plants in the middle and the little ones on each side, so that it looks quite all right from either side. Here is a plan for it:

VIRGINIAN STOCK		VIRGINIAN STOCK
CANDYTUFT	POT MARIGOLDS	CANDYTUFT
CORNFLOWERS	MALLOW	SHIRLEY POPPIES
CLARKIA	MIGNONETTE	CLARKIA
VIRGINIAN STOCK		VIRGINIAN STOCK

In case you are lucky enough to be able to buy a few *plants* for your garden, here are the names of a few flowers that you will be able to get cheaply to border your bed: pansies, double daisies, forget-me-nots, white arabis, mauve aubrietia, and pinks. Any of these will do well if bought at the beginning of April and planted out.

CHAPTER VI

A FEW CLIMBERS

IF YOU have a wall at the back of your garden you
will like to grow a climber there. There are many
climbers, all of them lovely, and most of them easy
to grow. Even if you have no wall you may like to
put some sort of trellis on the north side to make a
good background for your flower-bed, and also to
keep off the cold winds. Up this trellis you may
grow any climber you wish. Sweet peas may be
grown up sticks, as you know.

First, I will tell you about annual climbers you

34

may grow from seed. There are quite a number of these.

Climbing Nasturtium—This needs better soil than the Dwarf or Tom Thumb nasturtium. In fact, all climbers need a certain amount of care where their roots are concerned, because they have to make a great deal of growth, and to do that they need plenty of room for their roots and good soil to feed in.

If you are planting a climber, dig a big hole where the roots will be, and put a little manure far down, if you have any. Then fill up the hole with as good a soil as you have. When the climbing plant begins to grow, its roots will rove about the good soil, which will soon be enriched by the manure, and, finding plenty of food to feed on, will send up strong, healthy shoots, full of flower-buds. Do not plant too near the wall, because if you do the rain will not get at the roots, and the plants will grow feebly.

The climbing nasturtium will make a quick, thick growth and will soon cover your wall, fence, or trellis, hiding completely what is supporting it. Its bright flowers will make the back of your garden very colourful. Sow the seeds 2.5 centimetres deep and 7.5 centimetres apart. Then, later on, pull up the weaker plants and use the strong ones, one plant to every 22.5 centimetres. They will not choke one another then. You will find that a few sticks with strands of string or wire stretched across them will give your nasturtium the support it needs.

Canary Creeper—This is a very quick climber, and will cover your fence or wall with its pretty, canary-coloured flowers. It will also grow up a post or stake, and will completely cover an archway if you plant the seeds each side of the arch.

Morning Glory—Sow the seeds in May. The morning glory has pretty trumpets of white, pink and blue, and grows very quickly, twisting itself tightly round its support. If you grow it up a wall, you will have to stretch netting over the wall surface, as otherwise it will have nothing to hold on to. Like the climbing nasturtium, it needs something to help it upwards. It can reach a height of 3 metres.

Sweet Pea—Any one can grow sweet peas, but not every one grows them at their best. Where will you grow them? At the back of your garden in a row? Or in two or three patches to grow up into a pillar of flowers? If your garden is small, you will do better to have two or three small patches growing up circles of sticks, or grow the dwarf forms.

If you want a row of sweet peas or have room for a small hedge of them, it is best to prepare their bed in the autumn. This you can do quite easily. You must dig a trench where you mean to plant them. At the bottom of the trench you must put some old manure, as deep as you can. The roots of the plants will not grow down to this until the hot summer days, and they will be very glad to find it then. That is all the preparation needed.

Then, in April, sow the seeds. Make the ground

firm before you put in the seeds, but not too hard. Make little holes 7.5 centimetres apart, and about 5 centimetres deep. Drop a seed in each. Cover up.

They will soon grow—but enemies will be waiting for them to appear. The sparrows will come to find the seed and nip off the shoots, and the slugs will feast on the tender green leaves. Put down slug pellets, available from your local garden centre, but remember to wash your hands thoroughly afterwards.

You can keep the sparrows away by sticking twigs into the ground and winding black cotton between the sticks, over the sweet pea seeds. The sparrows will not come near when they find that their legs become entangled in the cotton, and your plants will grow in safety.

As soon as they are 5–7.5 centimetres tall, get some small twigs and put them by each plant. The plants will use these for support until they are ready for bigger stakes. When they are nicely grown, give them stout tall sticks, well branched. These sticks must stand 1.8 metres *out of the ground*, so they will be very tall indeed. See that they are very firmly set in the ground, for winds will come, and you do not want your row of sweet-peas blown over just when they are flowering nicely. You can buy the sticks, or collect them quite easily if you live near woodland.

If you grow your sweet peas in rows, place the sticks outside the rows, angled inwards so they meet at the top, so that each row of sticks braces the other. The sweet peas will grow happily up the stakes, feeling out for each little twig with their curling tendrils. If you are growing the sweet peas in a circle (six seeds to a circle) put the sticks round the circle on the outside and slope them together to meet at the top. Then you will have a fine pillar of flowers later on, covering the circle of sticks.

Sweet peas like plenty of moisture, so if the summer is dry you must water them well. You will find that it is quite a good idea to lay grass cuttings from the lawn all along the foot of the sweet peas, and this "mulch" as it is called, keeps the moisture in. Also you must remember to keep the flowers well picked, for if once you allow them to make seed the plants will consider that their duty is done and will fade away and die, instead of continuing to flower for many weeks more.

It is best to delay sowing any annual climber until the end of April.

Now I will tell you of a few climbers that will come up year after year, once they are planted. Try to buy young plants, as these will flower sooner than those grown from seed, and be sure to prepare the bed at the foot of your wall, fence, or trellis just as carefully as for an annual climber.

A FEW CLIMBERS

The Everlasting Pea—Some people are very fond of this old-fashioned flower. It is like a small sweet pea, but the colourings are not so lovely. There are many blossoms on one stem, maybe a dozen or more. It grows up to 3 metres high and looks well growing over an arch or up a trellis. The blossoms are usually pinkish or white. It is a useful climber to have if you want one that is quite able to look after itself. This plant dies back every autumn, but will reappear the next spring.

Flame Flower—This is a beautiful thing, one of my favourite climbers. You will find it in your catalogues under the name of *Tropæolum speciosum*. If you live in Scotland, you will probably know it well, especially if you live in a peaty district, for it loves peaty soil and thrives in a cooler clime than the south of England. It likes its roots to be cool, so plant them deep down—7.5–10 centimetres down if you live in Scotland, and twice as deeply if you live in the south of England! If the roots are too near the surface they will shrivel away and die. It is a good idea to plant the roots in a place where other plants will shade them. As soon as it has put out shoots, the climber will grow quickly above the other plants and cover the wall as high as you please. It blazes out into a marvellous mass of scarlet blossom, really like a great flame licking the wall. Everyone will admire it if you grow it well. It will die down in the autumn and grow again the next year. The great thing to remember is to plant the roots deep down, and keep them cool!

Clematis—This woody climber, with its large and pretty starfish-shaped flowers, is easy to grow. It likes rich soil, and please plant the roots fairly deeply. If you want an early-flowering clematis, you must ask for *Clematis montana*, which will flower in May, covering your fence or arch with a mass of lovely white flowers. If you would rather have a late-flowering clematis, get the lovely *Clematis* "Gypsy Queen", whose big blossoms are a deep rich purple. If you would rather have a white one, you can get *Clematis* "Marie Boisselot". I think you will find that the purple one gives you more pleasure, it is so rich and velvety. Remember that the clematis, like the flame flower, prefers to have shade when it is first growing.

Jasmine—There are two kinds of jasmine for you to choose from, the summer-flowering one, and the winter-flowering. The white jasmine, which has a sweet smell, flowers in summer, and covers a wall or trellis very prettily with a cloak of drooping green. It prefers to be warm and sheltered. The winter jasmine is yellow, and is very charming. It flowers in the middle of winter, when there is

40

nothing else in the garden save perhaps a few Christmas roses. It has lovely lemon-yellow flowers, very bright and clean-looking. As there are no leaves when the flowers bloom, the yellow blossoms on their wiry green stems are very decorative, and look lovely when cut for your bedroom or classroom. The leaves shoot out later in the year.

Virginia Creeper—I have only told you of flowering climbers, but if you should simply want a climber to cover something with leaves, you can get Virginia creeper, which you are sure to know, because in the autumn all the leaves turn to a brilliant crimson and scarlet, blazing away in the autumn sunshine as if they were alight. The Virginia creeper does flower, of course, but the blossoms are small and not noticeable. It is a very useful climber for a bare and ugly wall (the side of a house, for instance). For your own little garden, however, I should choose a climber with plenty of showy flowers.

CHAPTER VII

BEFORE I go any further I think I will give you some hints about such things as weeding, watering, and so on. You may think they are easy enough—so they are, but it is interesting to do them the right way, and to know why one way is right and the other wrong.

Thinning out your Seedlings

After your seeds have been sown for a month or five weeks, you will see that they have sprouted into a mass of tiny seedlings. Although you did your best to plant them thinly, they seem to have come up all crowded together. This will not matter in the case of the Virginia stock, which you want for a thick edging, but all the other plants need to be thinned out.

42

Now you must do your thinning out carefully. Here is a patch of candytuft, we will say. There seem to be about a hundred little plants with their stems all close together. Did I hear you say that it seemed a pity to pull any up? Well, we must, because if we leave them all to grow, they will choke one another, and you will get poor, feeble flowers that will die off very quickly. One fine plant of candytuft will give you a better show than twenty tiny ones—so we will harden our hearts and set to work.

You must pull out the smallest and weakest seedlings, leaving the stronger ones. It is difficult to do this without also pulling up or loosening the seedlings nearby. Therefore you will find it a good idea to water the seedlings well the night before you thin them out. If you do that, the seedlings will come up out of the earth easily, and will not much disturb the others. Pull a seedling out with one hand and keep the fingers of your other hand firmly on the earth by those you wish to leave. That will prevent half a dozen others from being loosened at the same time. If by any chance you do pull up or loosen seedlings you wish to leave in, you must make the earth very firm around their roots, or they will wither away and die in a short time.

When you first thin out your seedlings, leave a distance of 7.5 centimetres between the remainder. Now leave them for a week and then look at them again. You will find that they have made very good growth because you have given them space and air

—but they are already touching one another again! Thin them out once more so that there is a good space between the plants. They are really beginning to look like proper plants now, aren't they? Are there any buds?

Look at them once more in another week's time to see if by chance they have grown too thickly together, and take away any that seem to you to be feeble owing to being squeezed by the others.

Now you know all about thinning-out! It is very simple to do, and very important. If you don't thin out your seedlings, you will have a disappointing garden. If you do, every one will come and exclaim at the fine plants you have managed to grow! And they will probably say, "But you must have had very special seeds to grow plants like these!" They will hardly believe you when you say that it is only because of your careful thinning-out.

Transplanting

You may not have to do any transplanting this year, but you ought to know how to do it. Transplanting is the lifting of seedlings or plants and putting them somewhere else. You will probably look at the seedlings you have taken out during your thinning work, and think what a pity it is to waste all of them. Well, if you like to plant them somewhere else, they will grow into good plants and give colour to some little bare space elsewhere.

I don't expect you will have any room at all in your own garden to put these thinned-out seedlings

—but you are sure to find some bare places in your parents' garden which would be just right for your seedlings. I expect your father and mother will be only too pleased to have a few of your plants here and there in the beds.

The chief thing to remember about transplanting is that the little plants will be very thirsty, so, if you can, put them into their new places after a shower, or at any rate water the place well with your can or hose. Look at the little plants often during the next week and give them water if they need it. Plant them in the late afternoon or evening, if you can, then they have the cool night to help them. Let the roots spread out nicely as you put the plant in its new hole, which you have made with your dibber.

Do not trouble to transplant seedlings of Shirley poppies, mignonette, or love-in-a-mist, as these rarely do well when moved.

When transplanting a big plant from one place to another, water it first—then lift it with a trowel, taking care not to hurt the roots.

Hoeing

Good gardeners say that if we use the hoe well in the warm weather our gardens will not want much watering. Why is that? Well, the water deep down in the soil is always finding its way to the surface and escaping through the small spaces there. If we can prevent that, we shall keep in the earth the moisture that the roots need. By using our hoe well, as often as we can, we create a dust mulch which acts as a blanket and prevents the moisture from escaping (or evaporating, as it is called). So be sure to use your hoe often in the summer, and you will find that when your neighbour's plants are drooping and need water, your own are sturdy and fresh. Your hoe is making the soil keep its moisture!

Hoeing is also excellent for keeping down small weeds, the ones that root themselves near the surface. If you hoe them up, you may safely leave them in the hot sun to wither, but as you want your garden to look tidy, it is better to collect them when hoed up, and throw them away, or put them on your compost heap.

Hoeing also keeps the soil well aired, and prevents it from becoming caked together. The plants will like the finely-broken-up earth, so well stirred by your hoe, and will throw out good roots, making fine strong plants for you.

Watering

Even though you may keep the hoe going all the summer through in your garden, you will find that there are times when you must water. Watering can often do more harm than good, so be sure you know all the tricks of watering.

First, the best time for watering is in the evening. Never water in the hot sun. The flowers welcome water in the evening, for then they may drink every drop, but if you water in the sunshine, the sun will steal a great deal of the moisture, and half your watering is wasted.

Then be sure not to chill your flowers by giving them ice-cold water out of the tap or from a well! If they are hot with a day's sunshine, it will do them harm to chill them suddenly. The best water to use is from a rain-butt, or greenhouse tank, or from a pond, if you have one in your garden. Warm tap water is perfect.

What kind of rose has your watering can? (You know what a rose of a can is, don't you? The rounded thing that screws on to the spout of your watering can.) Look at it and see. Are there very many fine holes—or a few big holes? It is really best to have a can with two roses—one a fine rose for watering seedlings, if necessary, and the other a coarser rose with a few big holes, for watering bigger plants. If you have a hose, it should have an adjustable nozzle, to give you a fine misty spray for watering seedlings, as well as a coarser, stronger spray for other tasks.

When watering seedlings do it gently, or you will swamp them out of the ground, and it is a bad thing to make them loose about their roots. To water bigger plants, you must remember that it is the roots that are thirsty, not the leaves, and so you must hold the spout near the roots and water the ground there, not the leaves of the plant. If the plants are very big indeed, or you are watering a bush or young tree, or maybe a climber, take off the rose from your can, and water straight from the spout. Do not hold the can high up in the air or you will find that the force of the falling water disturbs the soil too much and may even lay bare the roots. Water with the spout near the ground. Stop every now and then to let the water soak in, otherwise it will simply run off the surface and do no good at all.

It is not a good thing to water while the hot sun is on the plants. If you do that, some of the drops left on the leaves of the plant may act as a magnifying-glass to the sun's rays, and may burn a piece of the leaf. You have perhaps seen a magnifying-glass catch the light of the sun, and send a bright spot on to a piece of paper. Very soon that spot turns brown and may even burst into flames! A drop of water on a plant may act in the same way, and you will get a disfigured plant as a result.

It is better to water thoroughly once a week or twice a week than to sprinkle your garden each day. If you give merely a sprinkle, the water cannot sink very far down. The top roots sense the water and grow upwards to get it. Next day the surface is baked hard in the sun and the poor surface roots shrivel away in the heat and die! A good soaking means that the water drains right down to the bottom roots, and all the roots feast on it and keep deep down in their proper place.

Sometimes in the evening you may put on your fine rose and water the leaves of the plants to give them a cooling bath. If you have a dusty garden this makes your plants fresh and clean-looking.

Mulching

Some gardeners mulch their plants to keep the moisture in the soil. A mulch is simply a spreading of something like grass-cuttings, leaf-mould, well rotted compost or manure. When a plant is watered and the moisture has soaked down, a mulch of grass-cuttings may be laid thickly round the plant's roots. This will prevent the moisture from evaporating, and the roots will be nice and cool. When you water, you must scrape away your mulch, and only put it back again when the watering is finished. As I said before, sweet peas will be glad of a mulching of grass-cuttings in the hot summer days.

Staking

Some of your plants are going to grow very big. When a high wind comes they will be blown over and perhaps broken, unless you stake them in time. You must stake any plant that needs it—for instance, a well-grown plant of cornflower is sure to need a stake, or you will find the whole plant on the ground one day. The best stakes to use are natural ones—sticks that you can cut yourself from a hedge, such as hazel. They don't show as much as white sticks or bamboo canes, which are very noticeable in a small garden. A green stick does not show very much, and you may be able to borrow some from your parents. Garden centres sell wire plant supports, which are very useful and don't show, once the plant is fully grown.

When you run your stick into the ground to stake your plant, be careful not to drive it down too near the root, or you will kill the plant. Set your stake firmly, for the plant will pull heavily on it in the next wind.

Tie a piece of string or raffia round the stick, then make a loop round the stem of the plant, so that the stem is not tightly wedged against the stick but has plenty of play in the wind without being too loose. If the stem rubs too closely against the stick it will injure it. You can also use plastic-coated ties, which are sold at garden centres. These ties come in different sizes, and you can join several together to make a long tie.

A big bushy plant may need two or three sticks round it, with a piece of raffia stretched from one to the other to prevent any of the flower stems falling down. A plant that is going to grow taller and taller will need a stick bigger than itself when young, and you will have to keep tying it here and there as it grows higher. Always try to stake a plant so that it still looks natural. It is ugly to tie a plant so tightly to a stake that it looks deformed or much too crowded together.

Picking off Dead Flowers

A plant sprouts, buds and flowers with one single aim—and that is to make seeds so that it may go on reproducing other plants like itself. Once a flower has succeeded in making seed, it cares about itself no longer. It drops its petals, droops, and dies—and very soon the plant turns brown and dies down too.

Now if we pick off all seed-heads, and all faded flowers, the plant cannot make seed. It knows its duty is not done. How can it do it? Why, by producing *more* flowers to try and make seed with those!

But again we pick off the fading flowers before they can make seed—and once again the plant grows a fresh supply of buds and tries to make seed! Thus, by continually picking off seed-heads and old flowers, we may make our plants flower for us week after week.

Our sweet peas will flower into October if we do not let the plants form seed-pods. But if we are away for three or four weeks, and the plant makes seed—then we shall find the sweet pea plants dying down in midsummer before they have given us nearly as many flowers as we want. Lupins will flower again, and so will the lovely delphiniums, if we cut off the old flower-heads. Cornflowers will go on for months, and so will pot marigolds, pansies and violas. In fact, most flowers will have a longer blossoming season if we carefully take off all fading flowers and never let them form seed. Our gardens will, of course, look much tidier, too, if we remove all old flowers.

CHAPTER VIII

A LITTLE VEGETABLE GARDEN

I AM SURE you will want to grow vegetables and salad if you have room. It is so nice to grow something you can eat for tea! Perhaps you have a big enough garden to divide into two, one half for flowers and one for vegetables. Or perhaps your parents will give you a little extra piece just for vegetables. One little boy I know grows quite a number of lettuces, runner-bean plants, mustard and cress, and radishes, and sells these to his parents. With the money he buys all his seeds for the next year, both flower and vegetable, besides any new tools he wants. I am sure you would love to do the same.

However small your vegetable garden is, you can grow three or four things in it. You must prepare it well by digging, as I have told you in Chapter II. The following are the things I should advise you to grow, for they will not take up too much room, are easy to look after, and are most useful for the table: lettuces, runner beans, mustard and cress, radishes, mint, tomatoes, parsley. Now to grow them!

Runner Beans

These, as you probably know, like to run up sticks, poles, or arches. The scarlet runner is the best, and besides being a useful plant for eating purposes, it is also pretty in its growth, its bright scarlet blossoms showing up among the green leaves. You can let it grow to 1.8 metres and then ask someone to nip off the growing shoots for you, because you don't want it to grow any higher. If you cannot let it grow as high as 1.8 metres, nip off the top shoots when 45 centimetres high, as that will make the plants bushy instead of tall. Continue pinching off the side shoots, to keep the plant bushy. There are also dwarf runner beans, which remain short and bushy naturally.

Sow the big bean-seeds in May, about the middle of the month, or early June in cold districts. Read the directions on the back of the packet and follow them carefully. It is always a wise thing to read the instructions on every packet of seeds. You will learn a good deal that way. Sow the beans 5 centimetres deep and about 20–30 centimetres apart. If you put them closer together they will choke one another. Give them their poles or sticks when you sow them, for they will soon want to climb. Remember to water your runner beans well in hot weather.

Do not let the bean-pods grow too big before you

pick them, or they will be stringy. They are nicest to eat when young and tender.

It is a good idea to grow your runner beans right at the back of your plot.

Lettuces

Would you like to grow lettuces? They are so nice to eat at tea-time with fresh bread and butter and salt! There are two main kinds of lettuce you can grow. One is called cabbage lettuce and the other is cos lettuce. The cabbage lettuce has two types: the crinkly leaved iceberg and the smooth-leaved butterhead. Both like to grow close to the ground in a squat rosette, rather like a small cabbage. The leaves look pretty when washed well and set on a glass dish. The cos lettuce grows tall, and its leaves are smooth and long, not crinkled. It is a little sweeter to the taste than the cabbage, though both are delicious. There is also a loosehead, salad bowl lettuce, with no heart. You pick the leaves as you need them, and more soon grow.

Lettuce seed is very tiny, so you must mix it with sand or fine earth when you sow it. Sow it about 20 millimetres deep. When the seedlings come up, you will see that, although you have sown them thinly, they are still far too thick! As soon as they are big enough to handle easily, thin them out. You had better leave a space of 15 centimetres between each lettuce, and later on, when the plants have grown in size, you may have to thin them out again if you want really good lettuces. Thinnings will grow into good plants if planted somewhere else early in the season, but you must remember to water them well, or they will die. After April, transplanted lettuces usually "bolt" – that is, flower and run to seed instead of putting their energy into making leaves. Bolted lettuces taste bitter, so it is not worth transplanting lettuces in late spring or summer.

If slugs come to eat your young plants, put down slug pellets. You can also trap slugs in scooped-out halves of grapefruit or orange. Put these out in the evening, near your young plants. The next morning, you will find the slugs feasting on the peel, and you can pick them off and put them in salt and water, which will kill them.

If you do not wish to grow lettuce from seed, I expect you can beg a few plants from your parents or someone who grows lettuces and is thinning them out. No one minds giving away a dozen or so of thinnings, and, if you water them in well, they will grow excellently. You can also buy young plants from a garden centre.

Mustard and Cress

Of course you will grow mustard and cress, and I expect you have grown it already, either at school or at home. You may have watched it growing on a piece of wet flannel, or on a sponge. It grows quickly and well, and is very soon ready for eating. We will certainly grow it in our little vegetable garden!

Do you want to grow it in the shape of your

name? Most people like to do that. What is your name? Is it a very long one? Then you must grow the mustard and cress in your initials instead— otherwise all your garden will be taken up with mustard and cress.

You must sow the cress three or four days before the mustard, because it takes that much longer to grow, and you must, of course, have both ready to eat at the same time. They taste so nice together. Now, are you going to sow them in the letters of your name? Very well, this is how to do it.

It is best to have a border of mustard and cress outside your name. It looks much neater if you do, and your name will stand out well. Get your hand-line, and set it up to guide you in making a straight line for the top of your border. Under the string make a *very* shallow drill. It is best to make the drill by simply laying down under the string the handle of your hoe or rake. Press the handle down gently, take it up, and you will see a shallow depression or drill left there. We must not plant our mustard and cress deeply. Do the same for the bottom line, and then join top and bottom by straight side lines. There is the frame for your name, beautifully straight.

Now draw the letters of your name *very* lightly indeed in the frame. If your hands are very steady and you can trust yourself to write your name with the seed itself, you can make the letters with the seed straight on the soil, without bothering to draw them first.

Remember to plant after a rain-shower, or else water the bed thoroughly the evening before.

Some people cover their mustard-and-cress seeds with soil, very lightly. Others put down a piece of sacking, or a board, over the seeds, until they have sprouted about 15 millimetres high, when they take off the covering to let the seeds have air and light. If you do not cover your seeds with soil, you must pat them well into the earth with the back of your spade before covering up—and be sure that the ground is nice and wet.

You can peep under the board or sacking now and then to see how the seeds are getting on, and as soon as they are high enough, take off the covering. Then they will grow splendidly, and will soon be ready for eating. When you cut your mustard and cress, the stalks must be cut fairly close to the ground. The roots are left in. You can pull them up and throw them away.

You will be pleased to see your name shining out in green mustard and cress, neatly surrounded by a green frame! Everyone will want to come and look at it, and really it will seem quite a pity to cut it. But you will enjoy eating it for tea, I know!

Mustard and cress is planted thickly and is not thinned out. We do not want it to make big plants, because we eat it whilst it is still in the seedling stage.

Radishes

Radishes are delicious things to eat when they are young and juicy, so we really must have a row of them. The kind called "French Breakfast" is a good sort to have for summer growing. Do not plant thickly, and be sure you thin out well as soon as the seedlings are big enough to handle. The seed is so tiny that it is best not to cover it up, but pat it into the earth with the back of your spade. To prevent the birds eating it, protect it with strands of black cotton wound about a few sticks. Watch your radish bed carefully, and if you see any roots pressing on others, pull them up. They will grow round and red, and if you pluck them when they are young, they will be crisp and delicious, and not too hot. Keep them well watered in dry weather, especially before you are going to pick them, as the roots like plenty of moisture.

Tomatoes

You need rather a lot of room for tall-growing, cordon-type tomatoes out of doors, so you will not be able to grow many of these plants. But bush tomatoes, such as "Tiny Tim" take up much less room, and you could grow a little row of them.

You can buy plants quite cheaply. Tell the person who sells them to you that you want plants for out-of-doors growing. Plant them firmly in your garden and water them in. Bush tomatoes do not need staking, but as it grows higher and higher, a cordon-type tomato will need support, so stake it well.

Tomato plants soon begin to grow, and send out trusses of yellow flowers, one above the other. Pinch out the top of the tall-growing plants when you have four trusses. Also pinch out any little side-growths on the stem. Bush tomatoes do not need pinching out.

You will like to see the tiny green tomatoes forming and gradually turning red. If the summer is hot they will ripen well, and you must be sure to water the plants regularly. You will enjoy eating your tomatoes with salt and bread and butter for your supper!

Mint

This sweet-smelling herb is useful to have in your vegetable garden, and will grow for years all by itself, once you start it. You must beg a root from someone in March or April. Plant the root about 5 centimetres down, and then watch it slowly throw up purple-green shoots, which will unfold into sweet-smelling mint leaves. The underground roots will shoot out fresh runners, and by the end of the summer you will have quite a nice little patch of mint. You can gradually train it all around your bed, if you like. If your garden is very small, and there is no room for the mint to spread, sink an old bucket without a bottom into the ground, up to its rim. Fill it with earth and plant the roots in that. Use mint for mint sauce, or take a few sprigs into the house when you are having boiled new potatoes or young peas for supper. Mint in the saucepan will give them a fine flavour!

Parsley

You can grow this from seed. Get the moss-curled kind, which is really very pretty. Sow the seeds about 2.5 centimetres deep. Weed and water the bed carefully until the seeds sprout. Don't be worried if you see nothing showing for weeks and weeks! Parsley takes a long time to germinate. It may be seven or eight weeks before you see the slightest sign of green in your parsley bed. That is why you must keep the row well weeded. If you do not, the bed becomes full of weeds, and when the parsley does come up at last, it cannot grow because the bed is choked with weeds. Then, if you suddenly weed the bed, you may unknowingly pull up all your little parsley seedlings! So keep the bed as bare and neat as possible until the parsley shows itself. Everyone will like it in parsley sauce, and it is useful for putting round cold meats.

Thin out the seedlings to about 15-17.5 centimetres apart. Watch for flower-buds, and as soon as you see these, nip them off. You grow parsley for its leaves, not for its flowers. If you want it to last you all the winter through, pick the plants very closely in the autumn. Then they will send out a batch of new leaves which you may take to the kitchen in the winter. If you live in the north, you will not be able to keep your parsley through the winter, but then you may try planting it in a pot and keeping it on an airy window-sill. Water it well, and you will be able to pull leaves from it when needed.

These are all the plants you could try for your

first year, if your garden is small. If you are successful with them, as I am sure you will be, try others next year. A row of peas is exciting to have. Cabbages are easy to grow, too—but, dear me! What a gap they leave in a small garden when you have cut them for dinner! Still, you can try anything —it's great fun, and it's wonderful what you can do when you want to.

CHAPTER IX

ANNUALS, BIENNIALS, PERENNIALS

You ALREADY know what annuals are—plants that are sown, flower, and die all in the same year. Probably your garden will be all, or nearly all, annuals this year, for, as we already know, such flowers as candytuft, cornflowers, and Virginian stock are easy to grow and make a fine show in a small garden.

What are biennials? Can you guess? Perhaps the first syllable, *bi*, will tell you. A *bi*-cycle is a two-wheeled cycle, isn't it?—a *bi*-valve is a shell-fish with *two* shells—so a *bi*-ennial is a plant with two years of life, not one.

A biennial is sown one year, and flowers the next. It has time to grow into a good, sturdy little plant before the winter, and then when the spring or summer comes, it flowers beautifully. Such things as wallflowers, or Canterbury bells, are biennials. If we want to grow our own wallflowers, we should sow the seed in the open in summer-time, say May or June. When the seed comes up, we should thin out the plants until they are 15 centimetres apart. We should keep the beds well weeded, and then, in October, when the wallflowers have become sturdy little plants, we should plant them where we want them to make a fine show next spring.

In the early spring they will flower, and give a great deal of colour and scent to the garden. Then they will make seed, but before they have finished doing that we should pull them up and throw them away to make room for summer plants. We do not keep biennials beyond their second year.

Hollyhocks are biennials, and so are sweet-Williams, foxgloves, and evening primroses. If we want to grow them from seed we must not expect them to flower until next year. That seems a long time to wait, doesn't it?—so, I expect you will be better pleased with annuals, or with perennials that you can plant in the spring to flower the same year.

If you would like to try growing biennials, you will have to ask for an extra bed that you can use for a reserve bed. You see, you cannot very well use up the room in your show-garden for little plants that will take over a year to flower. Also, when growing, the biennial seedlings prefer to be in a cool bed, not one that is exposed to a hot sun. That is where a reserve bed is useful—you can plant the seeds there in rows about 22.5 centimetres apart, and keep the plants safely there until you can put them into your show-garden in the autumn, ready for the next spring.

A reserve bed is also useful for putting in primrose roots, bulbs, and so on, when they have finished flowering in your show-garden, and you want their room for other things. Pop them into the reserve bed, where they will be cool and shady, and they will make good growth in the summer, and be ready for their proper quarters again in the autumn.

Unless you can manage to have a little reserve bed somewhere I should advise you not to try biennials. Make do with annuals, and with perennials.

And what are perennials? Well, there is only one thing left for them to be! They are plants that live and flower for many years, and even when they are old they do not really die. We separate out their roots and shoots and replant the new young bits here and there—and each will grow into a fine new plant!

You will find that many things in your parents' gardens are perennials. The lupins that come up year after year, the big delphiniums, the aubrietia that cascades in pink and mauve down the rockery, the masses of Michaelmas daisies, the mauve catmint—they all come up year after year, bright and cheerful.

Perennial plants are very useful to have, as you can see. They do not need to be sown each year, as annuals do. They do not die in their second year as most biennials do. They will look after themselves, once planted, providing that you keep the hoe going in the summer-time, and cut them down well in the autumn.

Would you like to grow some perennials in your garden? There are all kinds, tall, medium, and small, so you can make your choice according to what space you have in your garden. In the next chapter I will tell you how to treat perennials, and which to grow. There are one or two things you must know, but once you have learnt them, you will be able to grow any perennial you please.

CHAPTER X

YOU CAN, of course, grow perennial plants from seed, but unless you have a reserve bed, or would like to plant the seed in boxes, it is better to buy, or beg young plants from your parents or friends. I will tell you later how to grow seeds in boxes, in case you would like to try it.

In the autumn and in the spring most people are digging over their gardens and looking to their plants. A great many perennials, such as Michaelmas daisies, have grown such enormous clumps that they are taking up too much room in the bed. The owner thinks that they must be lifted and divided. If you are there when this is done, you will see that the lifted clump consists of a woody old-looking middle, and clusters of new young shoots all round the outside. The gardener cuts away bunches of the outside shoots with their roots, and throws away the old middle bit.

The new little clumps are replanted. Each will grow into a fine new plant. Now if you ask for one of these little clumps the gardener will probably be very glad to give you one, for I expect there will be

66

far more than are wanted, and they may end their days on a rubbish-heap if we don't rescue them.

The little clump you have will make a fine plant by next year, and will give you masses of flowers to pick. It will grow bigger each year, and the time will come when you must divide it too!

Now we will suppose that you have been lucky enough to beg or buy some good perennial clumps —perhaps a lupin or two, a delphinium plant, a clump of Michaelmas daisy, a few roots of pink or a clump of pink thrift.

New little clumps of perennial plants that you have begged from your parents or friends are best planted in the autumn or spring. If your soil is very heavy and cold it is then better to plant perennials in the spring. However, I hope that, autumn or spring, you will be successful in your planting. If some one offers you perennial roots in the spring, accept them eagerly, and plant them straight away. Container-grown perennials that you buy from a garden centre or nursery can be planted any time, as long as the ground is not frozen or waterlogged. If you plant them in summer, though, you must remember to water them well and often so they don't dry out and die.

Look at the root you are planting. Is it big? Does it look as if it wants to go deep down—is it long and pointed? It is sure to need a good big hole if it is going to grow into a big plant, so first of all dig out your hole and make it wider than the plant itself, for you must not squeeze the roots in a hole too small for them.

How deep must you plant the root? Well, look at the old stems left on the plant and see if you can mark where the earth came up to before. You will probably be able to see the earth-mark, and can plant the roots so that the earth will come up to the same place again.

Now you have your hole dug out. Lower the plant gently into it, and then go down on your hands and knees and gently spread out the roots in the hole. Do not let them lie in a heap all together. Roots spread out in all directions in the soil, and when replanted they must be put as much in their natural position as possible. Otherwise the plant will take a long time to accustom itself to its new home.

Now you have spread out the roots correctly, shovel in some earth and press closely and gently about the roots. Then fill up the hole completely, and be sure to make the soil firm round the neck of the plant. Go and look at it again in a day or two, for if windy weather should come, perhaps the plant will have become loosened—and no plant likes that. All plants prefer to be firm about the neck!

If you are not sure where the earth-mark is on your new plant, ask the person who gave it to you how deep to plant it. Some plants like to be in a deep hole, others prefer a shallower one. We must please them, or they will not grow for us.

Water the plant if the weather should be dry afterwards. Should you get the roots at a time when you cannot very well plant them—because of school perhaps—dig a large hole, put the plants inside, leaning against the side of it, and cover them up well with soil until you can find time to plant them. They will be all right.

If you are planting a container-grown perennial, carefully remove it from its container first. You will know exactly how deep to plant it, as the soil surface of the plant should be level with the surrounding garden soil.

And now suppose that you want to lift one of your perennials, either to divide it or to put it in another place. You must be very careful, or you will hurt the root of the plant with your spade or fork.

Some plants have tap-roots—that is long, fleshy roots that pierce far down into the soil. These roots must not be broken. If you break them you will injure the plant and it may die. A lupin has a tap-root and so has the big Oriental poppy. When lifting plants like these, it is best to use a fork, for the spade may break the root in half. The fork will loosen the plant and will not break the root.

When digging up a big plant, be sure to place your spade or fork a good way outside the plant, not close to it, for it is easier to avoid injuring the roots then. Lift plenty of soil with the plant. The roots are attached to the soil, and if you bring up the soil too, and replant the roots with the same soil attached, the roots will not have to do so much hard work in their new home. They cling to the soil by means of their fine root-hairs, and if you tear away the earth from them you will break the root-hairs, which will all have to grow again. That takes time.

Some perennials have fibrous roots, like the roots of grass. Others have clusters of thickish roots, and others, as we heard before, have very long tap-roots.

You cannot, of course, divide a plant that has one tap-root. You can divide the ones with fibrous roots quite easily, for all you need to do is to work the roots apart until you have two or three plants instead of one. Others, such as polyanthus, which has a cluster of little thickish roots, must be cut cleanly between the various rosettes of leaves into two or three plants.

Plants that have made very big clumps should be lifted, and the middle should be thrown out, for you will find that it has become woody and useless. Use all the little outside clusters for new plants. They will grow well for you.

A small trowel can be used instead of a spade or fork for smaller perennials, when you wish to lift them. Remember to be careful to dig a good way outside the plant, and lift as much soil as you can with the plant.

CHAPTER XI

HERE ARE some perennials you may like to grow.

Primroses and Polyanthus

You are sure to know both these plants. The primrose is easy to grow, and its beautiful yellow flowers set in their rosette of crinkled leaves are lovely to see in the spring. Primroses do not like too hot or too dry a place, so grow them in a shady corner, if possible, or somewhere moist. Polyanthus are like coloured primroses, but grow many flowers in a bunch at the top of one stem, like the cowslip. Both plants are cheap to buy, easy to grow, and will give you extra little plants, called "off-sets", each year, if you like to divide them.

When they have finished flowering, it is best to put them into your reserve bed, or in some shady corner, because they make a lot of leaf in the summer, and take up a good deal of room in your

71

show-garden. They like to rest in a cool and shady spot for the summer, ready to be put back into your garden in the autumn.

Violets

Do you like these? You can beg a few runner-roots from a friend, I expect, or buy plants from a garden centre, and you will be pleased to see the violets flowering as early in the year as March. They like a sunny place in spring, when they flower, but they shrivel up if their spot is too dry and hot in the summer—so if you can, put them to join the primroses in the reserve bed or shady corner after flowering. You can divide the violet clumps when you lift them, and plant each separately. They will have become fine plants by the autumn, when you put them back again in your garden. Do not forget to water any plant that you lift and place elsewhere. It may need watering for three or four days after moving.

Lupins

The beautiful spires of lupin look lovely in the early summer. You may get white, blue, yellow, orange, or rose-colour. I should get a coloured lupin, for the white are not so pretty. They grow tall and may need staking. The lupin tree is like a bush lupin and has pretty, creamy-yellow flowers with a lovely scent. It is a pretty thing to grow, and likes a warm, sunny place.

Delphiniums

Do you know the tall blue delphinium? Its flowers are so brilliant that they seem almost as if they were enamelled. It is a lovely plant to grow. There are many shades of blue and mauve to choose from. Try to plant it at the back of your garden, for the delphinium will grow taller than you are. You will have to stake it well, for the wind may blow it down. You can also get shorter delphiniums, for the middle or front of your garden. These do not usually need staking. Slugs are very fond of the tender new shoots sent up by the delphinium in March, so scatter slug pellets all round the plant to keep these pests away.

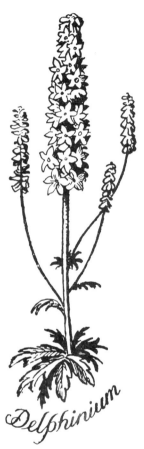

Delphinium

Michaelmas Daisies

What colour do you like? White, pink, blue, mauve, or purple? Go and have a look at the Michaelmas daisies in your friends' gardens in the autumn, and make up your mind which kind you like best. Then beg for a little clump of the ones you like, when they are being divided up, either in the autumn or in the early spring. They are graceful, decorative flowers, and they do not mind the autumn winds and rain. You can get low-growing, misty-looking daisies, tall bushes with strong spikes, or medium ones—there are enough kinds to suit all gardens!

Sunflowers

There are annual sunflowers, as you know, and perennial sunflowers. The perennial kind are very bright and pretty, but they are greedy flowers, and, if you let them, they will gradually send out their roots over the bed until they are growing over twice the space you meant them to have. So, if your garden is very small, say "no" to perennial sun-flowers. They grow very tall, and must therefore be put right at the back if you have them.

Pinks

You are sure to know the sweet-smelling pinks called "Mrs Simpkins". They are very easy to grow, and make a fine border for you all the year round, for they keep their pretty grey-green leaves in the winter.

If you only have a few plants, you can easily make more by pulling apart the roots, dividing up the shoots, then replanting them where you wish. You

74

will soon have enough for a complete edging to your garden! Pick off the fading flowers, and the pinks will send up a fresh batch of buds.

Columbines

These pretty, fairy-like flowers blossom early in spring. There are all kinds of colours. The old-fashioned kind have short spurs, but the modern kind have fine long spurs to the petals, and are dainty and beautiful. You can grow columbines from seed very easily, and by doing so may get some lovely colours. Be sure to buy good seed.

Pansies and Violas

The pansy is a great favourite. It really seems to have a little face, and a very pretty one, too! The big velvety flower may be all colours—browns, purples, yellows, white. You will love to have it in your garden. You can buy plants very cheaply in the spring, or you may raise your own pansies from

seed in July, putting out the little plants in your garden in October. The viola, or tufted pansy, as it is sometimes called, is also very easily grown, and will give you flowers from March to November.

You must remember to pick off all dead blooms from both pansies and violas through the summer, for if you allow the plants to make seed they will soon cease to flower. You may get new plants from your violas by breaking off a shoot below a joint and planting it firmly in the ground. It will send out roots and become a new little plant.

Chrysanthemums

Chrysanthemums are useful flowers, besides being

very pretty, because they bloom when there are not very many other flowers in our gardens.

You can buy young plants and plant them straight into your garden. They like a sunny place, with shelter from the cold winds. If they are well protected from the bitter winds you will be able to leave the roots in all winter, instead of lifting them and storing in boxes of soil in a frost-proof place. Leave 45-70 centimetres between the plants, for they will grow big. You will have to stake your chrysanthemums before the winds come, for the stalks are brittle and might break if bent too much.

Most chrysanthemums make bushy plants, but if yours do not seem to be sending out plenty of shoots, nip off the tips of the shoots. This will make the plant send out side-shoots, and it will become thicker and bushier. Cut the old stems down to the ground in the autumn when they have finished flowering.

You will find that your chrysanthemums send out many little new shoots in the spring-time, and you can get new plants for yourself by breaking off some of the shoots with the roots attached and planting them elsewhere. You may also increase your stock by taking cuttings; but this I will tell you about in another chapter.

Arabis

This plant likes to grow in a rockery, where it can spread out in a thick carpet, producing masses of white flowers in the spring—but you may, if you wish, grow it as an edging to your garden. You may buy young plants, or perhaps a friend will give you some cuttings. Trim back the plants after they have flowered, for they have a creeping habit and will become untidy. Cut off all dead blooms. You may increase your stock of arabis, if you wish, by breaking off any of the woody stems and planting the shoot afresh.

Aubrietia

This is another plant that loves a rockery home, but will grow very prettily as an edging. There are all shades of pinks and mauves, but the mauves, I think, are the prettier. Cut back the plants after flowering, as they make a great deal of growth, and if you use them as an edging to your garden, you do not want them to grow too far over the path. If you have them in a rockery, you may allow them much freer growth.

Alyssum (Yellow)

Yet another plant which loves to be in a rockery, but which will please you well as an edging, especially if mixed with mauve aubrietia and white arabis.

Double Daisy

All children like the pretty little double daisy. The plants are very cheap, and you may buy them

in the spring-time for your garden. An edging of double daisies is very pretty. Cut off all dead flowers and the plant will go on blooming for a long time. Water well in the summer if it needs it. Some people treat this plant as a hardy biennial, sowing it one year to flower the next, then throwing it away.

Dahlias

These are very lovely perennials, and if you wish to grow them, there are many things to know about them. I will give them a little chapter to themselves, so if you wish to grow them, please turn to Chapter XIII.

Foxgloves

If your garden is rather shady, this is a splendid flower to grow there. Many people treat foxgloves as biennials, but they will grow as perennials in a suitable place. They flower in June. You may get white, pink, or rose-purple kinds. The name is really "Folk's Glove", meaning a fairy's glove, and the flowers really do look like fingers of a small glove, don't they?

Geum

The geum likes a sunny place. It is quite a hardy flower, and if it likes your garden it will go on growing bigger and bigger each year, giving you masses of bright red or yellow blossoms. Cut them down when they are faded, and the plant will send you out a second batch.

Hollyhocks

These tall, stately flowers are usually grown as biennials, and are better as such. But some people use them as perennials, and in the right soil, in a sunny position, they do very well. They are not suitable for your garden unless you have a fairly large one, because they grow so very tall. They may grow 3 metres or more, and will need strong staking. The double ones are the prettiest.

Leopard's Bane

The other name for this early summer flower is *Doronicum*. I should like you to have a plant of this for your garden because it flowers so early, and will grow practically anywhere. It is very hardy, and will send you up many pretty daisy-like blooms, bright yellow in colour. You may see the buds forming in February, and a sunny March will bring the flowers out quickly. If you cut down old flowers, the leopard's bane will bloom again. Take some of the outer shoots in the autumn, and plant them elsewhere. They will make nice new plants for you.

Lily of the Valley

If your garden is moist and shady and has good soil, grow lily of the valley, that small and sweet-scented plant whose white flowers hang like tiny bells down the green stem. You will have to buy the roots or "crowns" in October, and plant them 5–7.5 centimetres apart. Cover them lightly with soil and, if you have it, spread 5 centimetres of leaf-mould over them, taking this away in the spring. Leave them for years in the same place so that they may grow and increase. If you want to divide your stock, do this in November.

Poppy

The poppy is called *Papaver* in catalogues. There are two perennial poppies you may like to grow. One is a small and very pretty one, called Iceland poppy. You may grow this from seed, when it will flower the second year, or you may buy young plants. You can get yellow, white, buff, salmon-pink, and orange Iceland poppies, and when mixed together in your garden they are very pretty. They will flower all the summer through. The Iceland poppy is a short-lived perennial, and some gardeners treat it as a hardy biennial or half-hardy annual, which I will tell you about later.

The big Oriental poppy is a magnificent fellow. Like all

81

poppies it loves a sunny place, and will more or less look after itself. As the Oriental poppy grows to a great size, give it plenty of room in your garden, if you wish to grow it. You may get white, scarlet, crimson, or orange. The scarlet is the brightest of all. Cut off all blooms when over. When picking poppies for indoor vases, pick those in bud, before the sun is on the bed, or after sunset—otherwise they will fall at once.

Phlox

Phlox makes a very bright patch in the garden in late summer, and is a very useful plant to bring colour to it then. It is also useful for picking. It likes a certain amount of sun and an open place, but does not like strong winds. You must remember to stake your plants of phlox fairly early. Also, look over the plant and cut away any thin, weak-looking shoots, so that all the strength of the plant may go to making fine heads of flowers on the strongest shoots. You may get white, mauve, and all shades of pink or scarlet.

Sweet William

This is another plant that is usually treated as a biennial, and is really best grown so. But you may grow it as a hardy perennial if you wish, providing you cut down the shoots that have flowered each year, and let the new little shoots grow. You may make new plants for yourself by dividing up the roots.

Snapdragon

The catalogue name for this pretty flower with the "bunny mouth" is *Antirrhinum*, but you are sure to know it by the name of snapdragon. If you open its "mouth" it will snap shut, which is why it has such an odd name. These flowers are grown as half-hardy annuals or short-lived perennials. They like to be in a sunny place, and do not at all mind a dry spot, for they will grown on the tops of walls, or in rockeries, and will seed themselves in gravel paths or between crazy-paving cracks. You may grow the plant from seed or buy it cheaply as small plants in the spring. There are tall kinds (90 centimetres–1.2 metres), medium-sized kinds (37.5–75 centimetres), and dwarf kinds (15–37.5 centimetres), so you will have a good choice. The scarlet, orange or crimson colourings are the best to have in a small garden, as they are very bright.

Pick the stems of the old flowers and you will see that the plant sends out many new flowering shoots.

The snapdragon will last until November, and give you plenty of blooms for your vases and jars.

There are many other perennials you may like to try another year, or if you have them given to you, but the ones I have chosen to tell you about are the kinds you may safely get for yourself and try to grow.

I will tell you about bulbs, corms and roses in other chapters. They need special treatment and understanding. Dahlias also shall have a special section to themselves.

CHAPTER XII

GROWING SEEDS IN TRAYS; PRICKING OUT

THERE ARE a great many pretty annuals you can grow if you have a frame or a greenhouse where you are allowed to keep your trays of seedlings until the weather is warm enough to plant them out in the garden. These annuals are called half-hardy because, although they are hardy enough to put out as plants in May or June, they are not hardy enough to sow in the open ground in April or May, as we do with other annuals, such as candytuft or cornflowers, as they cannot withstand frost.

The handsome zinnia, the pretty mauve ageratum,

and, in northern counties, the sweet-smelling alyssum, are some of the half-hardy annuals we can start in trays. Many perennials, too, are started in trays or pans, when sown as seed.

You are sure to like to know how to grow seeds in trays, and how to prick them out. It is great fun to try this, and is an excellent thing to do on a rainy day when you want to garden, but will get wet through if you do.

Spend an afternoon in the greenhouse or in the potting-shed, if you have one, and you won't at all mind hearing the rain pelting down on the roof. In fact, you will rather like it.

For sowing half-hardy annuals you will need trays or seed-pans. Plastic seed trays, with holes for drainage, come in different sizes and colours, and are really quite cheap. Some come with clear plastic covers and can be used as propagators. Or you can buy special heated propagators, into which several seed trays fit nicely. You can also use little peat pots, which you plant directly into the garden, without disturbing the plant it contains. And of course, you can use plastic or earthenware flower pots. Shallow ones are best. You can get good results with so many containers, even little yoghurt pots with holes punched in the bottoms.

At the bottom of your pot put a layer of broken "crocks" (bits of broken plant-pots) to help the drainage. You do not want your soil filtering out of the holes or cracks when you water the boxes or pots! The crocks will stop that, and the water will drain out clean. Seed trays are shallow and don't need crocking.

You must have good loam-based or peat-based compost for your seedlings. Be sure your pots, if you use earthenware ones, are clean before you put in the compost. It is best to wash them well with soda and water (hot) and leave them to dry, before using. If they should be old pots, any disease that the previous plant had will be given to the new seedlings, and you do not want them to be unhealthy.

Fill the box or pot nearly up to the rim, leaving about 2.5 centimetres to the top. Smooth the compost down with your hand. Water it through the finest rose of your watering-can.

Now sow the seeds. If very tiny, as are snapdragon seeds, mix with a little fine soil or silver sand before sowing (you can buy silver sand from builders' merchants). You may sow them in February or March. Your propagator, frame or greenhouse should keep a temperature of about 16°C (60°F) to make the seeds grow well.

Put a sheet of glass over each tray or pot, or put the cover on the propagator, if you have such a thing. It helps to keep in the moisture, but it is not really necessary. Some people also put a sheet of brown paper over the glass to keep out the light. If you do use glass over your boxes, you must be sure to turn this every day, because you will find that drops of moisture collect on the underneath of the glass, and these must be wiped off, or your seeds will be too moist.

As soon as the seeds are up, which is usually in about three weeks' time, take off the glass and the paper. You should not need to water your seeds at all until they have germinated. If the weather is warm, you may water your seedlings in the evening. If the days are cold, it is best to water before lunch-time, in case the seedlings should "damp off" and die, from remaining wet in the cold night air.

Now for the next thing—pricking out. I always like doing this, and I am sure you will enjoy it too.

Pricking out means lifting the tiny seedlings from their first pot or seed tray and planting them carefully at a certain distance from one another in other pots or trays. Why do we have to do this? Why cannot we leave the seedlings to grow where they are? It is because, no matter how thinly we have sown them, they always come up far too thickly to be allowed to grow together. So we must thin them out and replant elsewhere.

A great many people spoil dozens of their seedlings by lifting them the wrong way when pricking out. They pull them up by a finger and thumb, and so break or injure the roots. Seedlings which are to be pricked out must be lifted by means of a sharp-pointed plastic label, the kind that gardeners use for labelling pots or seed-beds. Water the seed tray or pot first and then the seedlings will come up readily. Do not prick them out until they are easily handled. After lifting them, plant them in other boxes, from 2.5–7.5 centimetres apart. Do not let the leaves of two plants touch. Plant the seedlings so that the first pair of leaves just show above the soil.

You will find that a pencil makes an excellent

dibber for you to make small round holes in which to insert the roots of the seedlings in their new box. Look at your seedlings. How long are the roots? Not very long? Well, then, make your hole not very deep, for if you plant a seedling into a hole which is deeper than its roots, there will be an "air-pocket" underneath, and this will cause the tiny roots to wither away.

To prevent this, you must make the soil very firm all around the seedlings, not only round its neck, but round its roots too. How are you to do this? Well, take your pencil and ram it down around the seedling three or four times, so that you press the soil close up against the whole length of the roots and make the plant really comfortable. Water the plants when necessary.

Soon you may "harden-off" your seedlings. This you can do by opening the greenhouse windows more and more, or, if your seedlings are in a frame, by opening the frame covers or "lights" wider and wider, so letting in more and more air. If you raised them indoors in a propagator, take the cover off for more and more time each day.

Then, when warm weather comes, you may stand your trays or pots of seedlings outside in a sheltered place—not only sheltered from the cold wind, but also from a too-hot sun, if the weather is really warm.

If frost threatens, you should close the windows or lights, and bring the trays or pots indoors overnight.

In May or June you may plant out all your half-hardy seedlings, which will now have become strong, sturdy plants, ready to flower.

Some half-hardy annuals you may grow in this way are the following: asters, stocks, French marigold, African marigold, nemesia, sweet scabious, tobacco plant, ageratum, sweet alyssum (which will, however, grow like a hardy annual in the southern counties of England), cherry pie, lobelia, and zinnia. I will tell you a little about each of these, in case you want to grow them.

China Aster

You may get this flower in all shades of pink and red, in mauve, and in white. There are single asters and double asters. Both are beautiful, but the single aster is more decorative and is better for cutting. They are very useful flowers to have in your garden, because they come into flower in the autumn when your garden may be beginning to look rather dull and colourless.

Ten-Week Stock

This useful flower usually blooms about ten weeks after sowing, hence its name. There are single-flowered stocks and double-flowered. The double-flowered are the ones to plant out, but, as they will not show you whether they are double or single when you plant them out, you must look at the leaves. If the leaves are long and pale green, the stock will have a double flower. But if the leaves are deeper in colour and stiffer, the flowers will be single, and you can throw that seedling away. There are tall stocks and small ones, so choose which you want before buying the seeds. These flowers have a very sweet scent and are lovely for cutting.

Ten-week Stock

Marigolds, French and African
(*Tagetes* in your catalogues)

Both these pretty marigolds like a warm and sunny bed. The African marigold grows about 45 centimetres high and has enormous globe-like flowers of orange and lemon. They last right into November and are splendid for cutting. The French marigold is smaller, but very pretty. Cut the flowers well, and they will go on blooming freely.

Nemesia

This is a dainty and charming flower, very suitable for your garden. Get a packet of mixed seeds, as one of the charms of this flower is the mixture of delicate colourings. It grows about 30 centimetres high, so do not put it too far back.

91

Tobacco Plant (*Nicotiana* in catalogues)

Do you know this plant that smells so sweetly in the evenings? You usually see it in white, but there are other colours—pinks, crimsons, violets and a lovely lime green. The white kind smells the best. The flowers open in the evening, and scent the whole garden with their strong fragrance. They grow about 60 centimetres high.

Scabious

The annual sweet scabious, or, to give it its pretty and descriptive country name, the pincushion flower, likes an open, sunny border. It grows from 45 centimetres (dwarf kind) to 75 centimetres (tall kind). Get a packet of mixed seed, for then you will have a lovely range of colours—cherry red, lavender, pink, peach, white, and bright scarlet, besides a curious purple-black shade. These flowers are lovely for cutting, and your parents will be delighted to have a bunch from you.

Ageratum

A pretty blue-mauve flower which looks like a big fluffy cushion when blooming. It is a splendid plant for an edging and looks very pretty mixed with white alyssum. You may also get it in white. Get the dwarf kind if you want to use it for an edging.

Lobelia

Another lovely little plant for an edging to your bed. There are all shades of blue, and white. The dark blues are very lovely. The dwarfs only grow about 10 centimetres high, and the "compact" kind grow 15 centimetres. There is a pretty spreading lobelia for hanging baskets and window-box edgings also. It is called *Lobelia erinus*, "Pendula", and is usually a glowing blue with a white eye. There is also a purple-red sort with a white eye.

Sweet Alyssum

As I have mentioned before, you may treat this as an ordinary annual if you live in a warm district, but as a half-hardy one, if not. It is a small, sweet-scented white flower that grows in big cushions of blossoms, and is splendid for an edging to any garden.

Zinnia

This is one of my favourite half-hardy annuals, a bold, bright, sturdy flower, with big pompoms of brilliant colour that make the garden bright from June to October. The zinnia grows about 45 centimetres high, and there are all shades of colour— bright orange, vivid scarlet, deep crimson, pure yellow, pale cream, delicate salmon-pink, flame, and even bright green. Get a packet of mixed seed and you will be surprised at the brilliant colours you see in your garden. The large double zinnias are the best to get. Water them well in the hot weather.

I wonder which of all these half-hardy annuals you will choose to grow! Begin them all in the same way, in pans or seed trays or pots in the greenhouse or frame, then they will flower early and make your garden bright for you. Remember to water them well after you have planted them out in the garden. The first few days in their new home are trying for half-hardy annuals, and you must look after them carefully. They will reward you with magnificent blooms.

CHAPTER XIII

ALL ABOUT DAHLIAS

SOME PEOPLE love dahlias so much that they like growing them better than anything else. They certainly are beautiful flowers, with their velvety petals, and their gorgeous, glowing colours. If you have only a small garden it is better to grow many things together, so that you always have something in bloom, and only one or two dahlias, or perhaps a small row of them if you can spare the room.

Dahlias are tuberous-rooted. That is, they have a base like a potato to grow from, but a different shape, and this tuber sends down roots into the ground. It grows bigger and makes other tubers, which, in turn, will give you fresh plants.

You may grow your dahlias from seed or you may get some tubers. If you grow them from seed, you must start them like half-hardy annuals, in a seed tray or pot in a propagator, frame or greenhouse. You can sow them in March. When the seedlings are ready to move, plant them singly in small pots. Put them in a frame, and then gradually harden them off by placing them outside on a warm day, and letting them stay out longer and longer.

Early in June you may plant out the dahlias about 60–90 centimetres apart. Plant dwarf forms 30–45 centimetres apart. They will flower for you the same year. As the plants grow, look and see how many shoots they are sending up. Cut off all the thin and weak ones. Stake tall dahlias firmly, and keep the plants trim and neat. Dwarf forms do not need staking. If you are anxious to have big, prize blooms, you must pinch out the top of the plant in early July, when tall dahlias are about 45 centimetres high. Do not let your plants grow more than six stems, and leave not more than one bud on each shoot. Then you will have enormous flowers, which may take a prize at a show.

But if you want many flowers, do not pinch out the top, and leave plenty of stems to bear flowers—eight or nine.

Water your dahlias about twice a week in hot weather, and do this thoroughly or it will be of no use. Do not give a sprinkling every day. That is harmful. Keep your hoe going round the roots. Look out for earwigs and slugs. Slugs will do a great deal of harm to the growing shoots unless you prevent them. You may catch a good many by putting an empty half-skin of orange or grapefruit upside-down on the bed. Look inside every day and you will catch the slugs. Put them in salt and water.

If you grow your dahlias from tubers, you may start these shooting by planting them in boxes of slightly moist compost in March or April. You must not plant them out in the garden until early in June. Harden them off first.

When the frost comes you will see that the leaves of your dahlias have turned brown or black. They will flower no more. If you live in the warm southern counties, and your dahlias are in a sheltered place, you may safely leave the tubers in the ground all the winter. Put a heap of ashes or sand over the tubers after you have cut the stems down. Leave them until the spring.

If you live in a cold district, you must dig up the tubers and store them away in a frost-proof place. Cut the stems down, leaving about 15 centimetres. Hang the tubers up somewhere to dry (with the stems pointing downwards) for a week, and then put them into a box of sand or ashes for the winter, so that no damp or frost will get to them. They will be quite safe, and you will be able to plant them again next year. Many people grow dahlias by taking cuttings of the new shoots in spring. When they are about 10 centimetres long, cut them off and put them in pots of compost. Once they have rooted, you can begin to harden them off, then plant them out when all danger of frost is over.

CHAPTER XIV

HOW TO CARE FOR YOUR ROSES

A SMALL garden will only take one or perhaps two roses, but they are so lovely in their colour, shape, and scent that you are sure to want to grow them at some time or other. They need more care than other plants, but they are worth all the attention we can give them.

We will suppose that it is spring-time and you have decided to have a rose in your garden. It is the month of March, quite a good month for planting a rose. You buy the kind you want, which may be growing in a container, or bare-rooted and sold in its own plastic bag. If you order a rose from a special rose nursery, it may arrive by post, bare rooted and packed in damp straw.

Look at it. You would never guess that in June that bundle of thorny sticks will be covered with the loveliest flowers in the world.

No frost must touch the roots. So, if you cannot plant the rose for a day or two, do not unpack the plant, but put it, just as it is, into the potting-shed or somewhere sheltered. It will be all right.

Now we will prepare the hole for it. Dig a wide, fairly deep hole, and not until the hole is ready must you undo the roots, for you do not want the air to get to the roots more than you can help, or they will dry up. Fill the hole full of water, and let it sink in. You may also dip the roots of a bare-rooted rose in water, too, if you like.

Now undo the plastic bag or straw from round the roots, which are all tightly huddled together. Look at the plant itself. Can you see the earthmark, showing where the earth came to when it stood in its previous place in the nursery garden? You must plant the rose so that the earth comes up to that mark, then it will be safe.

Use your secateurs to cut off any damaged roots, then spread out the roots. Put the rose into the prepared hole and see that the hole is big enough to take all the spread-out roots. Now shovel earth in, and make it firm over the roots. Fill up the hole. Tread down the soil firmly when finished.

If you are planting a container-grown rose, it is quite simple. Carefully remove the container, so you don't disturb the root ball. Place it in the prepared hole, making sure that the upper surface of the root ball and the garden soil are the same level. Shovel earth into the space beneath the root ball and the sides of the hole, and tread down the earth firmly.

Your rose tree is planted—but there is still something important to be done. You must prune your new rose tree hard—that is, cut back all its prickly branches so that it may make good growth and give you plenty of flowers. A newly planted rose is *always* pruned back hard, but afterwards you will not need to prune so mercilessly.

Pruning Roses

If you have roses you must know about pruning. You can, of course, ask your parent or another grown-up who knows about gardening to come along and prune your rose for you, but I am quite sure you would rather do it yourself. I would! It is easy when you know how to.

We prune roses for three reasons. First, we want to make our rose a good shape, trim and rounded, not one-sided or tangled in the middle. Second, we want to be sure that light and air can get freely to all parts of the rose, and therefore we must not let the branches grow too thickly or cross one another. Third, we want plenty of fine blooms, and pruning will give us them.

Now how do we prune? Well, we want a sharp knive, but if you are not very old you will do better to use a pair of sharp pruning-scissors, or a pair of secateurs. Perhaps your parents will lend you theirs if you promise to be careful with them, to clean them after using, and to put them back where you found them. Grown-ups are always willing to lend things to people who will give them back promptly.

Look at your newly-planted rose. Is there any dead wood that has gone brown or shrivelled? That must be cut right away. Then are there any weak or thin branches? Cut them away too. Are there branches that cross one another in the middle, so that, when the leaves come, light and air will not readily get to the middle of the tree? Cut away the branches that cross, leaving a nice open space in the centre. Now you have some sturdy, prickly branches left, and these must be cut well back until they are only 7.5–10 centimetres high. There won't be very much left of your rose then, and you may feel that you have been much too cruel to it—but you won't think so any longer when you see the fat leaf-buds sprouting next month and watch the roses coming into bloom in June.

You must cut the stems back at a special place, just above a bud—and you must see that it is a bud that points outward not inward, or you will find that you have inward-growing branches, and you must avoid that. Will you remember that? *Always prune a stem outwards and upwards just above an outward-pointing bud*. If you remember that, you will get shapely plants and strong ones.

Now your rose is pruned, and there is nothing more to do to it for a little while. Watch it and you will see that it sends out good strong tufts of red-brown leaves, tender and new, and the stem of these becomes longer and grows into a shoot.

When your rose is full of fresh new leaves, you must look at it each day to see that it has no greenfly on it. The greenfly love the tender leaves and buds, and once they take up their position on a rose they will multiply so fast that in a week's time every leaf and bud will be covered with the pest! They are fat, green, juicy-looking insects, and they feed on the juice of the leaves.

The quickest and easiest way of getting rid of them is to spray your rose with soapy water. If you have no sprayer and cannot borrow one, never mind. Get a large paint-brush and paint your roses with the warm soapy water. Keep a good look-out each day in case the greenfly appear again.

The Right Rose for your Garden

It is difficult to tell you which rose to choose for your garden, because a great deal depends on the district and on the soil. So the best advice I can give you is to tell you to ask at the nursery where you buy your rose, for one that will do well in your garden. The person will know the kind of soil you have and will sell you the best kind of rose for it. If you live in a clayey part of Kent, certain kinds of roses will grow marvellously for you and others not at all; if you move to Bucks, you may find that you cannot grow the same roses that did so well in Kent.

There are many kinds of roses. The two largest classes are called Floribundas and the Hybrid Teas. Some people call the Hybrid Teas "Large-flowered Bush Roses" and Floribundas, "Cluster-flowering Bush Roses". You may learn the different kinds and names when you want to grow more roses, but at present I only tell you this because different classes of roses need different pruning. Some roses must be pruned lightly, others less lightly, and yet others very hard indeed. Some must be pruned in March, others in April. It will only muddle you if I go into further details, and the best thing you can do when buying a rose is to ask the person at the nursery the following questions:

"Next year, when my rose is established in my garden, what is the best time for pruning it? How shall I prune it, lightly or hard? What is the name of my rose?"

Then the person will tell you what you want to know, and you must remember what is said. The tree will probably have a label round one of its stems with its name written on it. It is important to remember the name, because then if you forget what you were told about pruning, you can perhaps look up the rose in a gardening book, and there you will find the time of year to prune it, and whether lightly or not.

Remember to cut away the dead blooms as the summer goes on—and cut away also a good piece of stem with the rose, for the stalk will be of no use to the plant now. If you prevent the plant from forming seeds (the red hips) it will send up a second crop of blooms in the autumn, and these will probably be even better than the summer ones— deeper in colour, freer from greenfly, and more perfect in shape.

Roses like manure or well-rotted compost forked around them in the spring-time, so see if you can beg some from your parents.

The best time to plant new bare-rooted roses is not in March but in the early part of November, so that the plants have time to make themselves at home before the spring comes. But March will do quite well, so don't worry if your gardening only began this spring-time. Container-grown roses can be planted any time, as long as the soil is not waterlogged or frozen. If you plant them in hot weather, you must remember to water them well and often, to help them get established.

Always be on the look-out for dead wood in your roses all the summer through. Cut it out at once, or the branch will die back and back and infect healthy shoots. As well as greenfly, you must watch for caterpillars, for these may do a great deal of harm to the leaves and young shoots. It is annoying to see a lovely rosebud spoilt by being eaten at one side. Pick off and kill all caterpillars you see. If you see a hole in a leaf, look for grubs at once. *Something* must have eaten the leaf, and that something is probably still there!

If you live in a cold district, you must heap up the soil over the base of your roses in the winter, to give them a little protection against frost.

Climbing and Rambling Roses

If you have a wall at the back of your garden, you may like to grow a climbing rose up it, or let a rambler rose cover it with  masses of white, pink, or red blossom. You must not prune either of these roses as you do a bush rose. After ramblers have finished flowering, it is a good thing to cut away all the long sprays that held the flowers. This will strengthen the new shoots, which will grow tall and sturdy, ready to flower well the next year. With climbers, you should prune the side shoots to two or three buds back from the main stem, in autumn or winter. Cut out any dead wood too, of course, from rambling and climbing roses. This is all the pruning necessary.

A rambler rose likes to grow over an arch or up a post. The "American Pillar" rose, "Dorothy Perkins", or the "Crimson Rambler" will all grow strongly and well, giving you great tufts of brilliant blossom. Tie up the shoots when they grow long or they may become injured.

No rose likes too exposed a spot. Bitter winds prevent them from growing strong and sturdy. Bush roses do not like to be crowded by other plants, unless they are low-growing flowers, such as violas. Prune the roses well and care for them, and they will give you scores of beautiful blooms.

CHAPTER XV

HOW TO TAKE CUTTINGS

You will like to increase your stock of plants when you can, and you can do this by taking cuttings of many of them. It is fun to make three or four plants out of one, and it is quite easily done.

We will suppose that you want to increase your stock of pinks. Very well; in July, when the plant has finished flowering, go and look at it closely. Do you see that it has sent out three or four shoots or "slips"? Each one of these you can make into a new plant if you wish. This is how to do it.

Look at the stems of the plant. Do you see that here and there they seem to be jointed—they have bumps on the stem beneath the pairs of leaves? The place to cut away the shoot is just below one of those joints.

Choose a good strong shoot and cut it cleanly away beneath a joint. Take off the lower leaves leaving the stem bare.

Now go to your reserve-bed if you have one, or if not, choose a shady part of the garden. Take a pencil with you as a dibber, and, using the *blunt* end, not the sharpened end, make a hole about half as long as your cutting. Put a pinch of sand in the

106

bottom of the hole to help the cutting to make roots easily. Some people dip cuttings into hormone rooting powder before putting them in the ground or in compost. This helps the cutting to form roots quickly. If you want to use hormone rooting powder, you must be careful not to get it on your skin or in your eyes. And remember to wash your hands afterwards. Slip in the stem (about half the shoot should be in the ground and half of it out) and then make it firm in its sandy hole. Be sure the cutting is not loose in its hole, or it will not root. Water it well, and watch to see if it wants further watering later on.

In about three weeks the cutting should have sent out roots, and in the autumn you may plant the rooted cutting in your show garden, where it will grow and give you flowers the next year. You have a new little plant from your old plant!

That is how to take a cutting. If you wish to take many cuttings, you must prepare a cutting-bed. Dig a narrow trench and mix a good deal of sand with the soil. Then plant your cuttings there, watering afterwards. To shade the cuttings whilst they are rooting (they must not have hot sun, which would dry out the moisture in the leaves), you could pick a few branches of evergreens and stick them in the ground on the sunny side of the trench. That will give the cuttings the shade they need.

Cuttings of plants that are not very hardy are best started in pots of compost in a propagator, frame or greenhouse. Geraniums, for instance, will not root out of doors. Start them in the same way, in sandy soil.

Some plants are woody in the stem, and some are "soft" plants. When you take a cutting of a woody plant, put two thirds of the stem underground when "striking" it (as the rooting is called), but only about a half in the case of a "soft" plant. Always strip off the lower leaves before planting, or they will quickly rot.

If you are taking a cutting of a woody plant, such as lavender, see if you can take a little strip or "heel" from the main stem with the shoot, as usually this little "heel" will help the cutting to root more quickly.

"Soft" cuttings root in about three weeks. Woody ones take longer. A rose cutting may take a very long time indeed to root, but never mind. It will strike in its own good time, providing you have done everything you should for it. If the plant has no joints to guide you in your cutting, cut just underneath a pair of leaves.

Now I will tell you of a few plants you can take cuttings from, besides the pink, of which I have already told you.

Rose Cuttings

Would you like to try taking a cutting of a rose? Perhaps your parents have a rose that you very much like. Ask them if you may take a cutting from it. They may not believe that you can do this, but if you read on carefully, you will see that it is quite easy, and will be great fun. You will like having a rose that you grew yourself from a cutting!

108

HOW TO TAKE CUTTINGS

If you are taking four or five cuttings, prepare a narrow trench for them, filled with sand. Take the cuttings (in September or October) from the plants by choosing 20–30 centimetre shoots of well-ripened wood, which have borne flowers that year. Cut each off with a "heel" of the main stem. Cut off the shoot at the top down to the second leaf, and take off the rest of the leaves. Make nicks in the sandy trench with your spade and plant a cutting in each nick, leaving about 15 centimetres between each. Water in well, and continue to water regularly each day if necessary. Be sure to tread the earth very firmly around the cuttings, for they must not be loose. Plant them sideways, not upright.

They will send out roots in due course. The next summer they may flower, but it is best not to let them, or they will not grow as strong as they might. Pinch off the buds so that they will not bloom. By the following autumn they should be nice little plants ready to put into your garden for roses— your own growing from cuttings!

Cuttings will root in a frame or in pots if you prefer.

There is rather an amusing way of taking a rose cutting which you may like to try. Fill a medicine bottle with rain water. Take a rose cutting one summer day. Strip off the lower pair of leaves and put the stem into the neck of the bottle so that it touches the water. It should not touch the bottom of the bottle.

After a while you will actually see the rose stem sending out roots! Fill up the bottle with water as the level goes down. When there are plenty of roots, plant the cutting in some nice sandy soil, keep it well watered, and it will grow into a fine little plant.

Violas and Pansies

You may increase your stock of violas and pansies by the dozen if you wish. All you need to do is to take a small piece of root with a slip or shoot and plant it in good soil. It is best to take a young shoot, and when you cut it away make the cut as near the old plant as you can. The best time to strike violas and pansy cuttings is in August or September, though it can be done all through the summer and into autumn to the end of October. Strip off the lower leaves and plant as advised for pinks.

Dahlias

You may also take dahlia cuttings. Look at your dahlia tubers after you have put them in boxes of soil to shoot. You will find that they have sent out, in a few weeks' time, some strong shoots. When these are about 10 centimetres long you may cut some off and pot them up. When they have struck, you can put them out in a cold frame, harden them off, and plant them out in your garden in June, when they will make fine sturdy plants for you.

You now know enough about cuttings to be able to strike them from other plants, if you wish. Lavender, sweet William, rosemary, carnations, chrysanthemums, and many other plants will give you cuttings. Cut each one below a joint, or a pair of leaves, or with a "heel" of the main stem. Strip off the lower leaves. Plant well and firmly in a sandy hole. Water thoroughly. If you do all these things, your cuttings will always be successful, and you can get as many plants as you wish from those already in your garden.

CHAPTER XVI

BULBS IN THE GARDEN

SOME OF the loveliest of our flowers come from bulbs. You have all seen bulbs in the shops, and perhaps you have watched a grown-up planting them in bowls in the autumn. They are rather onion-like, with dry scales on the outside, and fleshy white scales inside. Right in the centre is the tiny flower with the leaves round it, all ready to shoot up when the time comes.

The crocus corm is different. It has its papery brown scales outside, it is true, but the corm itself is solid instead of being made of fleshy leaves, and the shoot containing the flower and leaves may be seen on top of the corm. But otherwise they are the same in the way they flower and grow.

112

BULBS IN THE GARDEN

You are sure to want a few bulbs or many in your garden. Which are you going to have? There are the bright yellow daffodils that "come before the swallow dares, and take the winds of March with beauty." There are the sweet-smelling hyacinths, with their enormous spikes of colour. Tulips, too, are very beautiful, so tall and stately. They flower in May and onwards. Crocuses are very early—they will begin to bloom in February. Snowdrops are earlier still, and the little yellow aconite will greet you at the end of January. Then there is the sweetly scented pheasant's eye narcissus, with its glowing golden eye—and the dainty little scilla, looking like a tiny bit of the spring sky, so deep a blue are the flowers.

I think you *must* have a few daffodils. And a border of yellow and purple crocuses is too lovely to miss! Then, of course, there are snowdrops—could you grow a patch of those, and perhaps a few blue scillas with them? It is difficult to choose, when you have a small garden and want so many things!

If your garden is really small I should get a dozen snowdrops and a dozen scillas and plant them together so that the blue and white are mixed. They will look very pretty. Then, if you can, get enough mixed crocuses to go along the front of your garden, two or three deep. Be sure to ask that plenty of *yellow* crocuses are mixed in, for if you do not, you may find that yellow is the one colour that has been left out. That would be a pity, because the yellow and mauve are so lovely together.

Then buy about a dozen or two dozen daffodils,

113

and plant them in clumps of six in your garden. If you have room, get as many tulips as you have money to buy and set them farther back, for they will grow taller than the other bulbs. You will be so pleased to see them flowering brightly in May. Ask for the May-flowering kind. If you want shorter tulips, for the front of your garden, some of the single and double earlies are only 25 centimetres high.

DAFFODILS & TULIPS

If you have only a small garden, that is all the bulbs you will have room for. You can try other kinds another year— especially I would like you to try the little aconite, with its buttercup yellow head and its pretty green frill just underneath. It is not a bulb, but it comes so early in the year that I must put it with them.

Now for the planting. Have you your bulbs ready? I hope you went to choose them yourself, because then you can handle each one before deciding to add it to your number. Bulbs that feel hard and firm to the touch are good ones. Soft bulbs are rotten inside and will give you no flowers, so do not take those on any account. Choose good-sized firm bulbs and you will have a splendid show. Always, if you can, buy your own flowers, seeds, and plants. People who do this are sure to get the best, because they see and feel what they are buying and soon learn to know what is excellent and what is third-rate.

Choose your bulbs early. The best ones go first, so you must not be late. You must plant them in September or October, so as soon as summer is gone, begin to think about what bulbs you are going to have. Make out your list, find out prices, and then go to buy.

Before you make up your mind about your bulbs you will, of course, go to your garden and decide exactly how much room you can spare for bulbs. If you wish you may pull up your bulbs after they have finished flowering and store them away until the autumn comes again—and therefore they will not interfere with your summer seeds.

Now we have all our bulbs in their bags. Can you tell which are which without looking at the name on their label or their bag? You can't? Well, just take a bulb from each batch and look at them all. That great fat round one must surely be a hyacinth! Its big spike of flowers needs a fat bulb. That rather untidy, straggling bulb which has perhaps two or three joined together, is the daffodil. The little round squat ones, very clean and neat-looking, belong to the crocuses. The thin small ones are the snowdrops. The clean, fresh-looking, rather reddish ones are the tulips. The pretty purplish ones, small and rounded, are the little scillas. Have you looked at them all? Would you know each one again?

You should have dug your bed well over before planting your bulbs, because you do not want to disturb them, once planted. Take your trowel and dig the holes for the bulbs. How deep are you going to plant them? Well, bulbs of different sizes need different depths. A good rule is to plant each bulb twice as deep as it is big. That is, if your bulb is 5 centimetres long, you should plant it in a hole 10 centimetres deep. If your bulb is only 2.5 centimetres in length, then plant it 5 centimetres deep.

The reason for deep planting is that the deeper we plant things, the less likely it is that frost will reach them. So, if you live in a cold district or far north, you should plant your bulbs deeper still— three times their own length, instead of twice.

Plant with a trowel, not with a dibber. A dibber will make a pointed hole, and when you drop the bulb into it there will be an air space beneath it which will wither the roots and prevent the bulb sending up good flowers. A trowel makes a rounded hole, which allows the base of the bulb to rest on the soil. Plant small bulbs fairly near one another, but the larger ones should be farther away. They must never touch one another. Plant them the right way up, of course. They will grow upwards whichever way you plant them, but those put in upside down will flower late because it takes longer for the shoot to grow to the surface.

Press the bulb firmly down in its hole. Cover up with soil. You had better mark where you have planted your bulbs in case you forget and dig them up by mistake when gardening.

Tulips should be planted late in October, because if they come up too early their leaves will be nipped by the frost. The earlier you plant your other bulbs the earlier they will flower next year, and the better flowers you will get, because the bulbs have had a good long time in which to prepare for blooming.

Planting Bulbs in Rough Grass

One of the best ways to plant bulbs is to mass them in rough grass, for they look their best blooming naturally there. The green grass throws up the brilliant colouring or dazzling whiteness of the flowers. Planting bulbs in rough grass is called naturalisation, and it is a lovely thing to do. For one thing, you do not need to take the bulbs up at all, but may leave them where they are for years, letting them grow and increase as they will. They make more and more bulbs or corms, which throw up increasing numbers of flowers, so that where a few score were planted you will get hundreds in time to come.

To plant bulbs in rough grass you must have your spade. Plan where you are going to put the bulbs first. Do not plant them in stiff groups. The best way to plant them is to make them look like a drift of flowers, with the thickest part of the drift in the middle. Take a good handful of bulbs and scatter them loosely on the grass. Plant them where they fall; they will then come up in a natural-looking group. With your spade nick out the grass you will have to lift. When you have nicked well all round the place, you will find that it is quite easy to slip your spade right underneath the turf and lift a big piece out bodily. Loosen the soil beneath with your trowel and plant the bulbs fairly deeply. Replace the turf you have neatly lifted and tread down firmly. Now do the same to another patch for a second batch of bulbs.

You must remember not to plant bulbs such as tulips, hyacinths and daffodils in a lawn. The grass of a lawn must be cut fairly early, before the bulb leaves have died down—and if the leaves are cut with the grass you will have poor flowers the following year, or none at all. The dying leaves are most important to the plant. They help to make the fleshy food-leaves of the bulb for the next year, so we must leave them as long as we can. You can plant crocuses in a lawn, though. Their leaves die back before the lawn needs mowing, and because they are small and grassy, you hardly notice them.

The best place for growing bulbs in grass is a bank that does not need to have the grass cut until early summer—or a wild place under trees—or in an orchard. If you have some place you know will be undisturbed, that is the ideal spot for natural-ising bulbs. Leave them there for years, and you will be delighted to welcome them every spring. They will flower very early indeed. Snowdrops, scillas, bluebells, and daffodils are the best for growing in grass. Tulips and hyacinths do not like it.

You may have to stake your hyacinths, so be sure to do it early enough before the wind blows the spikes over and spoils the flowers. No other early bulb needs support. You will probably have to protect your crocuses from the sparrows, who are very fond of nipping off the flowers, especially the yellow ones. To prevent this, do the same for your crocuses as you do for your seedling sweet peas— put a few sticks in the ground by your crocuses and wind strands of black cotton between them, over the flowers. The sparrows will soon avoid them and they will bloom unhurt.

Be sure to leave the leaves of your bulbs when the flowers are over, whether they are planted in grass or in your garden bed. You may think they look very untidy, and so they do—but you can easily knot the dying leaves neatly together so that they hardly show. They certainly do look very untidy if left all spread out and straggling, but they are hardly noticeable when knotted down. You may remove the leaves entirely as soon as they come away when you pull them gently. They will be yellow-brown then, quite dead. Their work is done and they can be thrown away. Far beneath in the soil is the new bulb or corm that the leaves have helped to make, all ready to flower in the next spring.

Once you have removed the leaves you have no guide to where your bulbs are planted in the bed. So you had better mark where they are by a stick or label, or you will find that in planting new flowers

LET'S GARDEN

you are digging up all your bulbs that you meant to leave for the following year!

Of course, if you would like to lift up your bulbs when they have finished flowering, you may do so—but leave all the leaves on so that they may finish their work. Cut off the dead flower. Now plant the bulbs in your reserve bed in a shady spot, and let them stay there until the autumn, when you may plant them in your show garden again. Some people wait until the leaves have died down before lifting their bulbs, and then, when the leaves have fallen off, they dig up their bulbs, put them into a box, and let them dry. Then they store them away in a dry, frost-proof place, dark and airy, until they are ready to plant them again. It is always best to lift tulips and hyacinths, and store them away when dry. Other bulbs may be safely left in the ground if you wish.

There are many different kinds of daffodils, of hyacinths, and of nearly every bulb. Some daffodils have long trumpets, some have short. Some are double, some are single. You may get tulips of all colours. Snowdrops you may grow, either double or single. You will have your own likes and dislikes, and a good catalogue will give you plenty of ideas as to what you may choose. Look through it carefully, read the descriptions of the flowers, and mark those you think you would like the most. Then go and choose them. There are a few other spring-flowering bulbs of which I have not told you, but these you may try at any time. There are many spring-times before you!

CHAPTER XVII

INDOOR GARDENING—GROWING BULBS IN CONTAINERS

INDOOR gardening can be just as exciting as outdoor gardening. More and more people are beginning to grow bulbs in bowls for the winter, and, if we do this properly, the results are marvellous. We get bowls of sweet-scented, brilliant flowers long before there are any blossoms in the garden.

I hope you will want to grow bulbs indoors. It is a very pleasant thing to do, and you will be very proud when your bowls are full of flowers. Visitors will admire them, and, if you are very successful, will ask your advice as to how to set about bulb-growing. I am sure that would please you!

You may grow bulbs indoors in four ways. You may grow them in fibre (which is the usual way), in compost, in stones and water, or in water alone. I will tell you exactly how to do it, and, if you will follow the instructions carefully, you will be certain to have beautiful flowers very early indeed.

Buy your bulbs for indoors in September. Choose good ones, firm and sound. As you will not want very many, it is best to buy really good ones so that you may be sure of getting the best results. It is not worth spending time and trouble on third-rate things. So choose the very best bulbs you can afford.

What have you chosen? Hyacinths? Daffodils? Crocuses? Tulips? All these will grow well in bowls, and so will scillas, and paper-white narcissi. If you want very early flowers, get some Roman hyacinth bulbs (the flowers are white) or some paper-white narcissi. You may easily have these in flower by Christmas-time, and will be very proud of them. Some bulbs, including certain daffodils, hyacinths and tulips, are specially prepared so they bloom extra early. These do cost a bit more, but really are worth it.

Now, have you bought any fibre too? You will want a bag of this—a small bag will do if you have only two or three bowls, but you will need more if you are going to fill many bowls and pots. The fibre is lovely stuff to use. It is made of peat fibre, broken shell, sand, and charcoal. Shake a little out into your hand and look at it. Put your hand into the bag and feel it. The beauty of using fibre is that it solves the problem of drainage. Bulbs grown in

fibre do not need a hole at the bottom of the bowl
to let the water out. The fibre will keep quite sweet
and good although there is no drainage, provided
you do not over-water.

Your bowls should be clean. Are they ready? Get
a big plastic bowl and empty into it all the fibre from
the bag. Make a hole in the middle of the heap (as
you do when you pour milk into a cake-mixture)
and then pour in some water till the hole is full.
Now mix up fibre and water with your hands. Mix
it well so that the water gets to every part. You
should make it damp all over, but not so sodden
that when you squeeze it water drips out. However
much you squeeze it, no water should appear.

Now half fill a bowl, if you are planting hyacinths,
or fill the bowl two-thirds if you are planting smaller
bulbs. Put the bulbs on the fibre, close to one
another but not touching. Fill up the bowl to within
2.5 centimetres of the rim. Firm down the fibre a
little. The tips of all bulbs should just show above
the fibre.

Finish all your bowls. When they are done, you
must put them away somewhere dark and airy until
the bulbs have made good root-growth. Unless they
grow their roots well they will not flower properly.
Have you a dark airy frost-free cellar you can put
your bowls in? Or a cupboard? It must be dark, and
it is equally important that it should be airy, and be
sure that you do not put the bowls anywhere warm.
I usually place mine in a dark corner of an airy
potting-shed, where they stay until they are ready
to come back into the house.

Wherever you put them, keep an eye on them. They will need watering now and again. Feel the fibre and you will at once know if the bowls need water. If it feels moist and cool, leave them unwatered. When you water them, return in an hour's time and tilt each bowl on its side, being careful to keep your hand on the fibre to prevent it falling out. Any surplus water will at once drain out, and you can safely leave the bowls, knowing that the bulbs are not too damp.

When you see that the bulbs have a pale green tip about 2.5 centimetres high, it is time to bring them out of the dark into our rooms. Do not put them into the strong light and sunshine at first. Put them into a dark corner for a day or two, and when you see that the shoot has become a strong, deep green then you may bring it to the light. Give your bowls a little twist each day, as plants try to grow towards the light, and if pots are not twisted round frequently the plants become lop-sided, which is very ugly.

If the weather is bitter and there are frosts at night, take your plants away from the window-sill, or you may find them frost-bitten in the morning, even though they are indoors.

If the fibre goes mildewy it is because you have watered it too much or the bowls have not had enough air.

A bowl of leggy, straggling plants also means that you have watered them too much or have stood them too long in a weak light. If the tips of the leaves or the flower buds go brown and wither, you have not watered your bulbs sufficiently. Do not let your plants stand in a draught. They hate that as much as we do!

Growing Bulbs in Pots of Earth

Daffodils will grow well in ordinary soil or soil-based compost, if you put them in pots that have good drainage—that is, a hole or several holes at the bottom. Get a pot and wash it well. Let it dry. Put a few crocks or stones at the bottom of the pot over the hole or holes. Half fill the pot with earth. Put the daffodil bulbs in, as many as you can without quite touching. Fill up with soil or soil-based compost to within 2.5 centimetres of the top. Water thoroughly. Put away in a cool, airy place. Then do the same as advised for your bulbs grown in fibre.

Bulbs grown in Stones and Water

Crocuses will grow far better in stones and water than in fibre. Collect some pebbles, not too large. Wash them. Half fill a bowl with them, putting them in layers. Now take your corms and put them neatly on the stones, close together. Pour water into the bowl so that it just comes to the base of the corms. Now just cover the crocuses with the rest of your stones. Can you find some green moss? If so, collect some from the garden and put it on the top of your bowl of stones. It will look very pretty there, and when the crocuses grow up between the moss you will be pleased. When the moss becomes dry (for the water in the bowl is too far down for it to reach), you must just take the pieces and soak them in water. Then, in a little while, when they are really damp and quite green again, you can replace them on the top of your stones. Or you can spray the moss with a sprayer filled with lukewarm water. This way, you can leave the moss in the bowl.

If you like you can sprinkle a few grass seeds over the damp stones. They will grow, and you will have a pretty carpet of grass and moss. I always scatter grass seed on the top of my bowls of fibre too, and by the time the bulbs are up the grass is green and thick, and the bowls look very pretty indeed. A handful of grass seed will be more than enough for you to use if you would like to.

The best thing about growing crocuses in stones and water is that you need not put them away in the dark. You may stand them straight away in the light, and have the joy of watching them grow from the very beginning! You will see them putting up their pointed teeth, as white as nuts, forcing their way between the pebbles, lifting the moss as they grow. Then from the white sheaths come green leaves, thin and spear-like. Then the brilliant flowers themselves, and how wide they will open in the sunshine they love! You may grow yellow and mauve together if you like. They may come out at different times—so, if you prefer, grow one colour in one bowl and the other in a second bowl.

Growing Bulbs in Water only

The fourth way to grow bulbs is to grow them in

water alone—no soil, no stones, no fibre, simply pure water. To do this you should get the special glass vases that are sold for the bulbs. These are called hyacinth glasses, and are tall and thin with a wider collar at the top to take the bulb. You may also grow crocuses in the same way, and you will find that they grow very well in acorn glasses, if you have any. You know the little glasses that you have for watching an acorn sprout into a little oak-tree, don't you? Most schools have them. There is a wide place at the top of the vase for the acorn, and here you may put the crocus corm instead, and watch it put out roots and shoots as it grows.

Fill the vase with clean water almost to the neck or collar. Put a piece of charcoal in the water and this will keep it pure. (You may take a piece of charcoal from the fibre you get for your other bulbs if you wish). Put the bulb in the top of the glass and see that it does not actually touch the water. The base of the bulb will at once sense that water is just below, and you will, in a few days, see tiny roots sprouting from the underneath part of the bulb down into the water.

As the water sinks, through evaporation, fill up the glass to the right level. Remove the vases from the window-sill on a cold night unless there is a curtain between window and vases.

As soon as the roots are growing well you will see the shoot pushing out at the top. The flower is tightly squeezed in the middle, and as it grows it will gradually take on its colour. It is interesting to watch both roots and shoot growing day by day.

The crocuses grow in the same way. A *purple* crocus usually grows best in an acorn glass. Yellow ones are not always successful.

When your Indoor Bulbs have finished Flowering

If you do not put your bulbs too near the warmth of a fire or radiator, you will find that they last in flower a very long time. They will scent the whole room with a delicious spring-like fragrance. When they are over, put them in a corner until the leaves have turned brown. Water them weekly still. Then take them out into the garden, find a nice shady place for them where you will like to see them coming up the following year, and plant them there. They will be of no use for planting in bowls a second year, but they will flower in the garden. You will not have very big blooms the next spring, but after that they will bloom beautifully. It is fun to keep a corner of the garden in which to plant out bulbs that have grown in bowls, for year after year the patch grows and is always added to. My corner has grown quite enormous now with tulips, daffodils, scillas, snowdrops, narcissi, and crocuses! It is the loveliest piece of the garden in March.

Kinds of Bulbs to grow in Bowls

Some of the best daffodils to grow in bowls are "Dutch Master", "Fortune" and "Mount Hood".

Any of those will give you splendid flowers. If you want the early paper-white narcissus, choose "Grandifloras". The white Roman hyacinth, as I said before, will also give you very early flowers.

If you like jonquils, choose the kind called *Narcissus* x *odorus campernellii*, which has a very sweet scent, and also comes into bloom early.

Among the best tulips to grow in bowls are the single and double early dwarf kinds, excellent for indoor growing.

Remember to plant different colours in different bowls. For instance, if you mix your hyacinths—blue, red, white—in one bowl, they will probably all come out at different times, which is annoying. But a batch of blue hyacinths in a bowl will all flower at the same time, and look very pretty indeed.

CHAPTER XVIII

COLLECTING YOUR OWN SEEDS

WOULD YOU like to collect some of your own seeds to grow next year? It is great fun to do this, and it will give you some work to do for your garden when the cold, wet days are here. Remember, though, that seeds of first generation (F_1) hybrid flowers and vegetables are very special, and expensive, and cannot be saved to sow next year. These you must buy each year from your garden centre. It is a good idea to keep your seed packets, so you can check whether the seeds are F_1 hybrids. It will say so, on the front of the packet.

If you want to keep some seeds for sowing, you must watch your plants and see which are growing big and sturdy, or are an unusual colour. Those plants which are healthy and strong, and which are making fine big seed-heads, are the ones to choose for your seed-collecting.

Suppose you want to take candytuft seeds. Choose the healthiest plants and let one or two run to seed. Soon, in late summer, you will see heads of flat-looking seed-vessels. Let them ripen well. They will go on getting drier and yellower. When they are brownish, flick the heads, and if you see a shower of flat, yellow seeds fly out, you will know they are ripe for you to take. On a dry, sunny day, pull up the plants by the roots and put them in a paper bag. Go to a sheltered corner (in case the wind comes and blows the seeds away) and shake out all the little flat seeds into your paper bag. Rub the heads between your hands to get out any that are left. Soon you will have a nice little pile of yellow seeds.

Get an envelope and carefully put into it all your candytuft seeds. Seal it up. There is your collection of candytuft seeds for next year! The plants will be strong and many-coloured.

You can do this with almost any seedling plant. Hollyhocks, for instance, will give you enough seeds to stock a thousand gardens! One hollyhock alone will give you hundreds of seeds. Let the seed-pods dry well before you take the seeds. You may cut the plants down, if you wish, and hang up the stalks to dry so that the seeds may ripen.

Poppy seeds may be shaken out of their round heads. The seeds will fly out as if you were shaking a pepperpot! Split the round heads of love-in-a-mist and take the seeds from inside. Shake out the seeds of snapdragons—there are hundreds of the tiny things! If you grow the giant sunflower, you will find that the ripening head supplies you with hundreds of pretty seeds, and you will only need a score, at most. So let the birds have the rest. Hang up the head from a tree-branch somewhere and watch the finches come and peck out the seeds. Their hard beaks can crack the seeds, and they will enjoy the kernel inside.

Put each kind of seed into a different envelope,

and pencil on it the name of the seed. Now, if you have a dull afternoon one winter's day when you really don't know what to do, and you are not allowed to go out and garden, finish off your seed-collection nicely.

You can either get a catalogue and cut out the pictures of the flowers whose seeds you have, so that you may paste them on to your envelopes, together with the printed name—or you may get your paint-box or crayons and paint or chalk the flower yourself. Print the name underneath. If the seeds in the envelope are big and make crayoning difficult, do the picture on a separate bit of paper and then paste it on the envelope.

Doesn't your seed-collection look fine now? There it is, as pretty as any collection of seed-packets in a shop. You will be quite proud to show it off.

Be sure to store your seed-packets in a dry place. It will be fun when spring-time comes and you can plant them all and watch the flowers that blossom from your very own seeds.

CHAPTER XIX

WHAT TO PLANT IN A SHADY BED

SOMETIMES children are given a part of the garden that is rather shady. Maybe there is no sunny piece available for them, or perhaps the grown-ups are not sure if the children are really serious about their gardening, and they think, "Well, no harm will be done if we give John or Jenny a piece under the trees there; that won't be noticed if the children neglect it or make a mess of it."

But never mind if you are given a shady garden instead of a sunny one. The thing to do is to make such a success of it that next year your parents will give you any piece you want because they are so pleased with what you have done with a difficult patch. Some boys and girls will not stick to a thing when they begin it, but you must always finish a job you begin, and, once you take up gardening you will want to go on with it to the very end—except that there isn't really an end to gardening, it's always going on. That, of course, is what makes it so exciting. Anyway, if you can only make a splendid success of a rather second-rate piece of ground, I am sure you will have no difficulty in getting a much better piece next year.

Now, what is your garden like? Is it always in the shade, or does it get sun for a little while in the day? Is it under trees that drip water on to the bed every time it rains? We will suppose that it is a very shady bed with dripping trees nearby.

First of all, go and look at your shady patch. Are there overhanging branches or jutting-out bushes that may be cut back neatly without harm? If so, ask permission and then with a pair of shears or secateurs cut back the bushy shoots. You may have to ask your parents to cut back tree branches. If you explain that you are trying to prevent the trees and bushes dripping harmfully on to your garden, they will be quite pleased to help you.

Now look at the bed itself. It will probably have been undug and untouched. So you must dig it well over yourself, just as I told you in Chapter II. If you have any manure, or well rotted compost, use that for the bottom of your trenches. The better you can make the soil, the better will your plants flourish.

Now, having dug over your plot and manured it if possible, and taken away every weed that showed itself, your bed is ready for planting.

I hope you will not be disappointed, but only a few annuals and biennials grow successfully in a shaded bed. These include the lovely forget-me-not, larkspur, love-in-a-mist and tobacco plant. You could grow these or spend your money instead on putting in bulbs and perennials that grow in the shade. They will give you splendid results, and later on, when by your success you have won for yourself a better patch, you can plant all the annuals you like in your new bed.

Many bulbs will do excellently in your shady garden. Snowdrops will thrive and multiply, crocuses will shoot up and flower brilliantly, daffodils will give you colour in March and April, and bluebells will carpet your patch with a mist of blue in May. Bluebells, as you know, grow thickly in the woods under the trees, so you can guess that they will thrive in a shady garden. They are useful and beautiful things to have, because they need no attention at all, and will increase rapidly each year.

The little blue scilla will also do well in your garden, and so will the graceful lily of the valley, which loves moist and shade. The winter aconite, that pretty, early flower, will show its golden face eagerly in the shade.

Other flowers that will grow well in a shady garden are primroses and cowslips. The primroses especially will make big yellow patches and flower profusely, for they are woodland flowers and like moisture and shade. Then there is the tall foxglove, also a woodland flower. It will grow well for you, and will look most decorative at the back of your plot. The columbine too (*Aquilegia* in your catalogues) loves shade, and will send up fine stalks of bloom early in the year. You will be pleased with the dainty flower, for it will grow well and make fine big plants.

Pansies and violas will grow at the front of your shady garden. Be sure to pick off all dead blooms or they will run to seed quickly and flower no more. The forget-me-not will also do quite well, as I have said before. When it has flowered and is running to seed, pull it up by the roots and throw it on a patch of the garden that is not used. The seeds will ripen and will fall out to the earth beneath. Then they will sprout and send up tiny forget-me-not plants. Take these up in the autumn and plant them in your shady bed. They will flower beautifully next spring, and you will not have to buy the plants.

Leopard's bane, or *Doronicum*, that early yellow, daisy-like flower, will also do well in a shaded garden. For an edging you could not do better than plant roots of that nice, old-fashioned plant, London pride. Do you know it? It has rosettes of stiff leaves, and sends up slender, sticky stalks which bear many small pink flowers. When you have a thick edging of London pride, it looks exceedingly pretty—like a pink mist. This plant does just as well in a sunny bed. In fact, it will grow anywhere, town or country, sun or shade.

Then there is the attractive plant called honesty, which you have already read about in the list of biennials. It loves shade and moisture, and will throw up its bright pink flowers early in the year, and then give you spikes of silvery moons in the autumn, which you can strip and take indoors for decoration.

Michaelmas daisies will not mind growing in the shade for you, and neither will that big graceful plant called golden rod. Do you know it? It has spires of bright yellow flowers at the top of a tall stalk, and goes very well with mauve Michaelmas daisies. You will find that it flourishes right at the back of your bed. You will have to divide up the roots after a time, or it will grow too thickly.

The little blue periwinkle prefers shade and will creep all over the place if you let it. It sends out beautiful soft-blue flowers, like bright eyes, between its deep, evergreen leaves. Then there it the yellow St. John's wort (the kind called *Hypericum calycinum*) which is useful in a shady place and will soon cover up the bed for you.

Solomon's seal is one of the prettiest of the shade-loving plants. It has long fronds of pretty, drooping leaves, and underneath you will see many creamy white bells. It loves moist soil and shade, and will send its creeping roots everywhere for you. It grows about 60 centimetres high.

Flags, or purple irises, do quite well in a shady,

moist bed. They are lovely things to grow, and beautiful for indoor decoration. They will send out their fat, creeping roots in a big clump once they are established. You will be able to divide them up and replant them in other spots.

There is one very attractive flower you may grow in your shady bed—one that is admired and wondered at by everyone; and that is the Christmas rose. As you probably know, it is not really a rose, but more like an anemone. It flowers just about Christmas-time or after, which astonishes people who do not know the flower.

If you would like to grow a Christmas rose, you must prepare a place in your bed for it. In the autumn dig a big hole about 60 centimetres wide and 45 centimetres deep. Now get some good rich soil and some old manure or well rotted compost. Mix it up and fill the hole with the mixture.

Buy or beg a plant of the Christmas rose and plant it carefully and firmly in the place prepared for it. It will soon feel at home and make itself ready for flowering. You must watch for buds in December, and you will be pleased when you see the fat round things pressing up from the centre of the plant. If the weather is very bitter you might put a flower-pot over the plant at night and take it away in the morning. You will be proud if you can take some Christmas roses into the house on Christmas morning. People will certainly think that you are doing well with your shady garden.

Ferns, of course, will love your moist and shady bed. Most kinds will do well there, and they will look very pretty as they open their green fronds. The Royal ferns (*osmunda*) will do very well for you.

Well, I have told you quite a host of flowers for a shady garden. You should be able to make a pretty, flowery place that will surprise your friends and parents. Try it and see what happens.

If your garden is terribly shady, almost sunless, just try the following plants: St. John's wort, ferns, periwinkle, Solomon's seal, snowdrops, primroses, and bluebells. You will not be disappointed with those. Make sure you water these plants well and often, because the trees or buildings that keep the sun off your plants may well keep the rain from reaching the plants, too.

CHAPTER XX

WINDOW-BOXES AND POT PLANTS

IF YOU have seen a house with window-boxes, I expect you admired it very much. Windows with a border of bright flowers are most attractive. The boxes are easy to buy and easy to stock, and if you would like to try making *your* window bright with flowers, I will tell you shortly how to set about it.

The best position for a window-box is facing south, but no matter in what direction your window looks, you may have a successful window-box.

Garden centres have window boxes of all sizes,

shapes and colours. Some are plastic, others are terracotta, fibreglass, wood or even concrete. Ask your parents to help you choose one. Measure your window-sill first, and remember to take the measurements with you!

When you get it home, put it in position and ask your parents to fix it securely, so it won't fall off the window-sill. Get some small crocks (broken bits of pot). You must have a layer of these at the bottom of your box, or, when you water the soil or compost in it, it will seep out of the holes with the water, and you will find your window-box gradually becoming empty of earth. Put a layer of fine nylon mesh on the crocks. You can use old cut-up tights. Now fill up your box with good fine soil or coarse peat mixed with charcoal, or soil-based compost, so that it comes to 5 centimetres below the rim. This is to leave space for watering.

It is best to put in plants twice a year when growing them in window-boxes. You can sow seeds in your box in April or May, or put in plants, which will flower for you all the summer. Take them out in the autumn, and put other kinds in the box, such as wallflowers, or bulbs, which will flower in the spring. Then, when *those* are over, they may be lifted to make room for summer plants once again.

A good many of the common annuals will grow well from seeds in your window-box. Candytuft, mignonette, pot marigolds, dwarf nasturtiums, and clarkia will all grow splendidly. Then if you like to frame the sides of your window in flowers, as well as the sill, you may grow a climber each side. Plant either the climbing nasturtium or canary creeper at the ends of your box. Run a string or wire up each side of the window for them to climb up—and in the summer your window will be a real picture!

There are many plants that like a window-box home. Choose only small plants, for tall plants look wrong and also take away the light and air from the room inside. Such plants as dwarf snapdragons, white marguerites, blue lobelia, yellow calceolaria, scarlet geranium, and bedding begonias, will brighten up your window and make it lovely to see. Violas, pansies, musk, and fuchsias will do well too, and they do not mind a shady window, so remember them if your room faces north, or lies in the shadow of another building.

For spring plants (which you will put in during the autumn), choose wallflowers, including the bright orange Siberian wallflower, which is very pretty indeed for a window box; aubrietia, which will hang down gracefully over the edge of the box; primroses, double daisies, polyanthus, and forget-me-nots. Don't forget that crocuses and daffodils and, later on, tulips, make a very brave show too.

Keep your window garden well weeded and watered. You will be surprised to see the number of bees and butterflies that come to it every day! Pick off the dead blooms, and your plants will flower all the summer.

Pot Plants

Some people like pot plants very much, and you may wish to try growing a few garden plants in pots. I have already told you all about bulbs in pots and bowls. Now I will tell you about seed plants.

Be sure your pots are clean. Fill with good compost after putting two or three crocks at the bottom. Water the compost, then sow a few seeds on the surface. Cover them lightly with a fine layer of compost.

It is best to have few plants in a pot rather than many. One or two plants will be sturdy and strong, but a number in a pot will be weak and straggling. So when your seeds come up, watch them and choose the strongest. Pull out the others. Leave only one plant in if you have a specially fine one.

Candytuft will grow well in a pot and so will the sweet-scented mignonette. Nasturtium makes a very pretty plant for pots. Clarkia, too, looks tall and graceful. You may grow two or three clarkia in a pot, unless you have a very fine plant you want to grow alone.

Water your pot plants regularly, and let them stand on a saucer so that surplus water may run out without making a mess. Empty the saucer when necessary. Do not let your

plants stand for long in a saucer of water. Keep them on a sunny window-sill, if you are growing them indoors. Make sure they get plenty of fresh air, though they won't like draughts!

You may also grow wild plants in pots. Try planting seeds of buttercups, knapweed, or chicory. The plants come up strong and sturdy and are really beautiful when in flower. Try them and see!

CHAPTER XXI

HOW A NEW FLOWER IS MADE

THE MAKING of a new plant is a very strange and wonderful thing. Do you know how it is done? I have said to you often in this book that flowers make seed, and once or twice I have mentioned that bees help to take the pollen from one flower to another. But I have not told you the whole story. Here it is.

First of all, pick some simple flower, such as a wild rose, a buttercup, or a poppy which is just opening and has not yet dropped its green outer coat.

Do you know what the parts of your flower are called? The under-part, the green leaves or coat that wrapped the flower up when it was a bud, are the sepals. (Fuchsias and some other flowers have sepals that are brightly coloured, and look like

145

petals!) Inside the sepals come the pretty, brightly coloured petals. Inside the flower is a ring of little stalked things, with powdery heads, the stamens. And in the very middle is a green thing which is probably sticky to your finger, called the pistil.

Pull away the stamens and look at the green centre, the pistil. Do you see that it goes right down into the middle of the flower—the part that will be the seed-box later on? The top of the pistil is called the stigma, its stalk or neck is called the style, and the lower, thicker part is the ovary.

I wonder which parts of the flower you think are really the most important. I expect you will say the bright, showy petals that attract the bees and flies! You would be wrong, if you did. The important parts, the parts that the flower could not possibly do without, are the stamens and the hidden pistil.

Why is that? It is because the stamens and the pistil together help to make the seed. The petals and the sepals are not really necessary for that. Indeed, many plants do without them—such as the grass, for instance, which never bother about anything but stamens and pistil. Perhaps you did not even know that grass flowered? It does—but because you see no bright petals you do not notice whether grass has flowers or not.

The pollen that flies from a stamen is in the form of very tiny grains. If you saw these under a microscope, you would see the pollen grains of each flower differed from the grains of another, and were very beautiful when magnified. You cannot see the grains with your naked eye—all you can see is powder that stains your hands or nose if you touch it.

Now every pistil of every flower wants a pollen grain to come to it. Not until a grain goes to a pistil can that flower begin to make seed; and as every flower must make seed if it can, the pistils wait day by day for the pollen.

When the stamens are ripe the pollen grains are set free. Sometimes the wind carries them away, sometimes a bee or a butterfly. You know how a bee pollinates a flower, don't you? I am sure you must often have seen a bee yellow with dusty pollen. The bee does not go to the flower for pollen—no, it goes for the nectar that the flower supplies for it. In return the bee unknowingly takes pollen from one flower to another. A flower—a poppy, for example—much prefers another poppy's pollen to its own. Seed produced from cross-pollination, as it is called, is much better than that produced from *self*-pollination.

The bee goes to the flower for nectar. It brushes up against the powdery pollen, and this is scattered on its back. Off it flies to the next flower, and as it seeks there for nectar, it rubs its back against the waiting pistil of that flower. It leaves a pollen grain or two on the sticky tip, then off it flies again, having done some very useful work without knowing anything about it!

Now what happens? The pistil has got what it wants—a pollen grain from another flower. Now comes a wonderful thing. The pollen grain knows that it has come to the right place. It puts out a tiny white tube, so tiny that we could not possibly see it with our naked eye. This tube runs all the way down the neck of the pistil until it reaches the ovary or seed-box. In this are waiting some small round ovules or half-seeds. They look like very small, unripe seeds, green and unformed. They will never be whole-seeds unless a pollen-tube reaches them. They are only half-seeds till then.

As soon as the pollen-tube arrives at an ovule it enters it. Once it has entered it the half-seed begins to grow into a whole-seed. Other pollen grains put out tubes down the pistil, and these, too, find little half-seeds or ovules and set about making them into whole-seeds. The seeds grow larger and larger. The seed-box or ovary has to grow too, or the seeds would burst it. So it, too, becomes larger, and we say, "Ah, this flower is making seed!"

When the seeds can grow no bigger, they are ripe. Then the seed-box begins to dry up and split, and sooner or later the seeds are shaken out, or fall out to the ground. What happens then? Why, if the weather is mild and the ground is moist, they germinate and grow! A tiny root springs out, and then a tiny shoot—and, hey presto, a new plant is born!

Isn't that a strange and interesting story? Now you will see clearly that it is the stamens and the pistil that are the most important parts of a plant. Petals and sepals do not matter. Why, then, do plants bother to produce them?

They grow them because by the bright colour of the petals, and their sweet scent, they attract the insects which will take the pollen from flower to flower! If the flower's pollen is to be taken by the wind, the plant does not bother about scent or colour, for the wind has neither eyes nor nose. But it must consider the insects, for they will not come unless tempted. The sepals, of course, are mainly for protecting the bright petals when in bud.

It takes two partners to make a seed—a pollen grain and an ovule or half-seed. If no pollen reaches an ovule, it remains a little half-seed and will never grow into a plant if you sow it. Have you ever seen any half-seeds? Yes, very often! Think of a pea-pod full of peas. When you shell them, do you sometimes see, at the ends of the pod, one or two tiny little undeveloped green peas? Those are ovules or half-seeds. No pollen grain reached them, so they could not grow into big fat peas like the others in the pod. They had to remain small and incomplete.

Hybrids are very special kinds of plants. Each parent is a different species, or different variety of the same species. Sometimes hybrids happen in nature—the delicious loganberry is a natural hybrid—but "cross-breeding", as it is called, is usually done by plant breeders, to get better and better plants.

There are many kinds of stamens and many kinds of pistils. Look into the middle of flowers and see how many different kinds you can see. You will be surprised at all the shapes and sizes! Watch a flower making seed, from the time its petals droop and die to the time when it stands with a ripened seed-head. You will not be able to see all the things that have happened, but you will know that one day a pollen grain came to the pistil of that flower, ran its tube down the neck of the pistil, reached a half-seed and began to make it into a whole-seed. The petals died because they were now of no use—but the seed-box grew and ripened marvellously, giving you many strong seeds to plant in your garden the next year.

CHAPTER XXII

SOME STRANGE THINGS EXPLAINED

Why do the Leaves Fall?

You must often have thought it strange that most trees throw off their leaves in the autumn. Why should they shed them and stand bare for so many months? For a very interesting reason!

Every leaf has a great many holes (or *stomata*, as they are called) scattered over its surface. Through these holes the water that is in the leaf evaporates and passes off into the air.

This passing off of water is a splendid idea in the summer, for then the roots of the tree can take in as much water as they wish and send it up to the leaves to replace any that is evaporated. But when the cold days come and the earth is frozen, the roots cannot take up any water at all. Then what will happen to the tree if all the water it possesses is rapidly given off by the leaves, without any being sent up to replace the loss? The tree would die.

"If I cannot stop my leaves throwing away my precious water in the winter, I shall have to send away the leaves themselves!" says the tree to itself. Then we see the limes and the beeches, the oaks and the birches, and many, many other trees flinging away their hundreds of leaves when the autumn winds come. Soon they are quite bare. All their water-wasting leaves are gone. The trees may rest for the winter and sleep soundly. Only the evergreens, those trees which manage to grow thick, tough leaves, or who make their leaves needle-like, so that little water can be given off, still hold to their leaves all the winter.

What makes the Leaves Fall so Easily?

This is another question I expect you have often asked yourself. It is strange that in the spring-time the leaves are so hard to pull off a twig, and yet in the autumn they fall at a breath of wind or a snap of frost.

The tree uses an excellent way of getting rid of its leaves. Up the tree run thousands and thousands of tiny bundles of water-pipes, and many of these bundles run from the twig into the leaves. They take water to the leaf. Now what happens if you pick up a leaf, put it into a jar, and give it *no* water? It shrivels up and dies! Well, the tree stops sending water to the leaves. It grows a little layer of cork over all the water-pipes just where they enter the leaf, so that no water can pass through. The leaf begins to die. Soon it snaps off because it is almost completely separated from the twig by the layer of cork. Down it goes, whirling in the air.

Look at the twig and see the place from which the leaf fell. Do you see the leaf-scar there? A horse-chestnut twig will show you plenty of scars in the shape of a horseshoe. Each nail in the little horse-shoe marks where a bundle of water-pipes entered the leaf. If you could find the leaf itself, you would see that the horseshoe pattern came from the shape of the leaf-base and that there were "nails" or water-pipes showing there too, exactly matching those in the horseshoe mark on the twig.

Why do the Leaves Change Colour in the Autumn?

Leaves change from green to vivid reds, yellows, oranges, and browns for a curious reason. As the leaves begin to die, they change from sober green to all the glowing, brilliant colours we know. Gardeners like to use leaves as manure, and dig them well into the soil, because they know that the leaves will dissolve into the ground and enrich it. So be sure to save your leaves and dig them into your garden.

What is a Fairy Ring?

How often have you asked that question, and had no reply, I wonder? A fairy ring is certainly a very strange thing to see. It is a round ring of toadstools

enclosing dark-green grass that stands out quite clearly in the lighter grass. How did it come there? Was it really made by the little folk for a dancing-ground?

This is how it came. One night a toadstool grew there. The grass was the ordinary colour, and there was no difference between it and the surrounding grass. The toadstool ripened and sent out thousands of spores—minute things that were scattered all round the toadstool in a ring. These spores in their turn grew up into toadstools, whilst the first toadstool gradually shrivelled and died. The ring of toadstools ripened and sent out spores in their turn. No spore that fell inside the ring ripened because the space and nourishment there had already been used by the first toadstool. So only those spores that fell outside the ring grew into another wider ring of toadstools, whilst the first ring died down into the grass.

Now as the toadstools died down and their juices soaked into the grass, the grass became rich, and flourished. It grew a deep, luscious green, and, because the toadstools had grown in a ring, so the grass deepened in colour in the shape of the ring—and then you came by and said, "Oh look! There's a fairy ring! I wonder how it came there?" Well, now you know!

What is an Oak-Apple?

What is the fruit of the oak? An acorn, of course. Certainly not an oak-apple. Then how did the oak-apple come?

An insect made it grow! It is a kind of insect-house, and its real name is oak-gall. You may sometimes have seen soft, pinkish-brown balls, spongy to touch and irregular in shape, at the end of an oak twig. Pick them and look at them. Perhaps you can see a little hole in some of them. That is the hole out of which the insect crept when it left the little house which had given it food and shelter all the summer through.

LET'S GARDEN

The oak-apple was caused by an insect coming along to the tree one day and making a hole in a stem. It sent down some poison and an egg, which made the oak-tree twig grow very quickly just at that place, and the growth formed a gall or oak-apple. In this gall lived the growing insect, which, when it was mature, bit its way out of the gall and flew away. It will fly to some oak-tree and start other galls in the same way as its parents did. The oak tree does not like this, because the forming of galls takes away much sap needed for the young twigs.

There is another oak-gall you may often notice on the oak-tree when it is bare. This gall grows in clusters of hard brown balls. They too were made by an insect.

What is Gossamer?

Those of you who like to go out in the early autumn mornings to garden will have marvelled at the silky strands of gossamer that are spread in hundreds over gardens, lanes, and fields. Where does it come from?

It is all made by tiny spiders going off on their first adventure! A young spider does not stay near the place where it was hatched out with its dozens of brothers and sisters. It prefers to go away and find a place of its own. So one autumn morning these small spiders set out. Each stands on a leaf or a post and sends out a long strand of silken thread. The breeze takes it up into the air, higher and

156

higher. The spider feels the pull, and when she thinks the strand will bear her, she lets go her hold of leaf or post and allows herself to be taken up into the air by her flying strand of gossamer. Up she goes, adventuring in the wind until she has gone far enough.

How does she get down to earth again? Very cleverly! She hauls in her thread little by little, and the shorter the strand gets the lower she falls. At last she sails gently to the ground, or to a hedge, and there she makes her new home.

That is the explanation of all the shining gossamer you see spread over your garden on a sunny autumn morning! Next time you find it, look and see if you can discover the tiny spiders that have made it.

Why does Mistletoe Grow on an Oak Tree?

Perhaps you have seen the queer dark clumps of mistletoe growing high up in an oak tree or springing out from an apple tree? You are surprised to see that it is mistletoe, whose pearly berries shine with the holly berries at Christmas-time. Why does it grow from a tree? Why does it not grow by itself, as other things do?

The mistletoe is what we call a parasite. It likes to take part of its food ready made from another tree. It is a robber.

It is mostly planted by the birds. A thrush will feast on mistletoe berries and will then go to clean its beak on a nearby tree. A seed rolls down a branch, and, because it is very sticky, does not fall off. It usually stays underneath the branch. Soon it sends out roots, called sinkers, into the tree branch, and these pierce right down into the sap. Then the mistletoe uses the tree's sap to feed itself, and soon a little pair of leaves appear on the branch—mistletoe leaves! Then more and more sinkers are sent down, and more and more leaves appear. Soon the mistletoe is a fine bushy plant, and bears flowers and then, later, pearly-green berries. We cut it down and decorate our houses with it at Christmas-time. But it is a robber-plant, a thief of another's sap, a parasite!

If you want to grow a mistletoe plant yourself, save some berries. Push them into a crevice on the lower side of an oak, apple, or black poplar branch. It will send down sinkers and grow!

CHAPTER XXIII

ENEMIES IN THE GARDEN

WE HAVE many enemies in our gardens, and, fortunately, many friends too. It is important to be able to recognise which are our friends and which are not. In this chapter I will tell you a list of insects and other pests which do harm to our plants, and how to deal with them.

Snails

Of course you know very well what a pest the slow garden-snail can be! It will eat your young plants, and will feast gloriously on lettuces and any other tender leaves. As snails leave a silvery trail

159

behind them, you can often trace the traveller back to his home, and you will find the snail under a stone, or hiding among the mass of leaves of some thick creeping plant, such as arabis.

Hunt for snails, if you suspect them of robbing your plants. When you find them, put them into a pail or tin and get an adult to pour boiling water on them. This kills them immediately and is the best and quickest way of getting rid of them. It is a pity to have to kill things, but if we are going to keep a garden, we must get rid of pests which would destroy it if they could.

Slugs

Slugs are also a great nuisance in the garden, and, like snails, they love a damp or shady place. They will devour all your tender young lettuces if they can, so be on your watch. You can pick them off your plants with a pair of small tweezers. Otherwise your finger and thumb will get very slimy and will be difficult to clean. Put boiling water on the slugs to kill them, or put them in salt and water.

To prevent them coming to your plants put a ring of weathered ash, salt, or lime round your lettuces or young plants. Neither snails nor slugs like this, and will avoid your garden if you continually use some preventative. You can also trap slugs with slug pellets, which you can buy at a garden centre. They should be scattered round the plants you wish to protect.

There is one slug, the testacella, which is a friend,

not an enemy. You will find it in the list of garden friends.

Greenfly

You are sure to have seen this green blight on roses or other plants. The dangerous thing about greenfly is that they multiply in so astonishing a manner. Where you saw three one day, you may see three hundred in two days' time, and three thousand in a week's time. A greenfly in time saves nine! So be sure to tackle your greenfly as soon as ever you see one, and save it from multiplying nine times, and more.

They are small green creatures, with fat, rather juicy-looking bodies. They have long feelers, very thin legs, and, if they have wings, these are fine and gauzy. But usually you will find greenfly without wings. Each greenfly is provided with a kind of beak for piercing the stem or leaf of the plant, and sucking up the juices. They also ooze out a sweet, sticky juice, and this, by closing up the pores of the plant, does it harm.

You may get rid of your greenfly by spraying them well with soft soap (available from your chemist) dissolved in water and allowed to cool. This drowns them and washes them off. Be sure to tackle your greenfly as soon as you see one or two. It is easy to destroy them when they are only a few in number, but difficult when they number thousands. It is a good idea to pinch off young shoots if they are covered with greenfly, using your thumb and forefinger. Spraying a plant with a strong jet of water from a hose also helps wash greenfly away, but you must do this again, every few days, until you are sure there are none left. If you try all these methods, and the greenfly still remain, ask your parents to buy a suitable insecticide, and apply it for you. Some insecticides will kill greenfly without harming friendly garden insects. Never, never use insecticides yourself.

Millipedes

Do you know a millipede? It is a quick-running creature with many, many legs. If you look at it carefully you will see that it has two pairs to each segment of its body. Centipedes, which are our friends, not our enemies, are not usually so rounded as millipedes, and have only one pair of legs to each segment. If you find a millipede and disturb it you will see it immediately coil itself up like a watch-spring. (A centipede runs for cover when disturbed.) There are many different kinds of millipede. Look out for them when digging, and if you see some, you will know that they are feasting on the roots of your plants, causing them to droop and die.

You may catch these enemies by burying a potato or a carrot in the ground. The millipedes will find it and burrow into it, eating it for food. You must dig up the potato or carrot at intervals, and drop the millipedes you find hidden there into a pail of boiling water.

One good reason for keeping our gardens well

dug over in the autumn is that in digging we bring many of these pests to the surface. The birds find some, and the frost kills the rest. A well-dug garden rarely has much trouble with enemies such as millipedes.

Daddy-Long-Legs, or Crane-Fly

The daddy-long-legs fly lays eggs in our soil, which hatch out into ugly grubs called leather-jackets. These feed on the roots of plants, then turn into a chrysalis and eventually emerge as daddy-long-legs, which begin the life cycle again by laying eggs in the soil. Digging our gardens well will help to get rid of this pest, because the sun and wind will dry out the grubs and kill them. If we encourage the birds to be our friends, they, too, will help us.

Other insects also lay their eggs in the soil, and their grubs damage the plant roots, or eat round the stem just where it emerges from the ground. If you happen to notice a plant injured in this way, take a stick and stir the soil round the plant. You will probably find the grub, thick and fat, hidden there. If you don't find it, very likely a robin will!

To prevent these grubs harming your plants you should bury carrot or potato, freshly sliced, in the soil about 2.5 centimetres deep. Kill them when you find them on the slices. Or you may put a flattish stone on your garden, and underneath place the slice of potato for a bait. The pests will come out to feed on it at night, and will hide under the stone during the day. You will find them there.

Woodlice

These are funny little grey things that coil themselves up tightly into black bullet-like balls. Slices of
carrot or potato will catch them too.

Earwigs

You may find that earwigs come to your dahlias,
hollyhocks, or chrysanthemums and harm them. If
you get a small flower-pot and put it upside down
on a stick, putting inside a piece of moss or some
straw, you will find that the pests go into the pot to
hide, and may be shaken into boiling water when
you find them. Drive the stick into the ground just
by the plant that is being infested. Earwigs love a
dark place in which to hide, and will choose the pot
at once. You will catch dozens that way. You can
also lay down hollow bean stems, and the earwigs
will creep inside at night. Every morning up-end
the stems into boiling water. Earwigs will even hide
under wooden planks or old sacking placed on the
ground.

Wireworms

You have probably seen these yellow creatures,
very highly polished, and cylindrical in shape. Their
skin is very hard, and they look and feel rather like
a thick piece of yellow wire. They are terrible pests
to have, for they do great damage in the soil by
attacking the roots of any plant they have a liking for.

They are the grub form of a beetle, called the click-beetle or skipjack. Do you know the beetle? There are many kinds of click-beetles, and they are all rather long-shaped, and usually green-brown or red-brown. The beetle itself prefers fallen leaves or decaying matter to growing plants, and so does little damage—but when it lays eggs that turn into wire-worm grubs, then great damage is done. The beetles get their name from the fact that when they happen to fall on their backs they are able to bend their bodies and then straighten them again with a loud click. They jerk themselves up into the air and, in falling, land the right way up.

Robins are very fond of the bright yellow wire-worm. They will perch close by your side when you are digging if they hope for wireworms to be turned up. They will see the pest long before you do, and with a flick of wings and a little chirp they fly down and swallow the grub at once. So encourage robins, for they will be a great help!

Digging over your ground well will rid it of wireworms (they remain in the grub stage for four or five years, and in that time can do immense damage), and burying potato or beetroot slices will also help to prevent the pest, for you will find them feeding on the bait when you dig it up.

Caterpillars

Caterpillars, as you know, are the second stage of the life of a moth, butterfly, or fly. First the egg,

then the grub, then the chrysalis, and at last the fly, butterfly, or moth, the perfect insect. It is best to get rid of caterpillars by hand-picking. Watch to see that none of your leaves or buds are being eaten. If you see holes in a leaf, or ragged edges, or if you see two leaves stuck together, examine the plant carefully. You will probably find a small caterpillar hidden beneath the two leaves, or inside a curled-up leaf, or perhaps underneath an eaten leaf. Pick it off and drop it into boiling water. Once you suspect caterpillars on a plant, examine it every day, for the caterpillar you first saw will probably be one of a batch, all of which hatched out at the same time, and are somewhere nearby eating all day or night long! If you grow cabbages and see the white cabbage butterfly about your garden, go and hunt for the eggs underneath the cabbage leaves. If you can find and destroy the eggs, you will save your cabbages. If not, out will come a horde of greenish-yellow caterpillars, slightly hairy, and marked with black spots. They will eat away all the cabbages and spoil them. There are certain insecticides that will do a thorough job of killing caterpillars, without harming insects and other creatures that are garden friends. If you have tried hand picking caterpillars, and find that more and more new ones appear, ask your parents if they would please buy such an insecticide, and apply it for you.

ENEMIES IN THE GARDEN

Sparrows

Sparrows are both enemies and friends to our gardens. They are enemies in that they come and steal the peas we have planted, or peck our crocuses and lettuces; and friends because they feed their young ones on grubs and caterpillars in the spring-time. It is easy to prevent them from doing damage by putting strands of black cotton or pea guards over our seedlings or crocuses. You can also hang strips of white fabric or aliminium foil on string. The strips flutter in the breeze and frighten away the sparrows.

CHAPTER XXIV

FRIENDS IN THE GARDEN

GARDENERS HAVE many natural friends. If they know them and encourage them to help, they will find that they do a great deal of good work.

Birds

Although sometimes birds do damage in the garden, the good they do far outweighs any harm; so you should make friends with the birds as much as you can, and encourage them to come to your garden.

You may do this by putting out a bowl of water for them all the year round; by giving them food in the winter, when they are hungry and it is difficult for them to find food; by supplying them with nesting material; by trying to tame the friendly robins; and by hanging up nesting-boxes for birds to nest in.

A bird-table is simply a flat slab of wood nailed on to a long post or pole, well out of the reach of a leaping cat. Spread this with household scraps, such as crusts of bread, bits of potato, fat, cold porridge scrapings, and so on, and the birds will visit your garden all day long. Hang up a coconut for the tits—a whole one, with an opening at each end. They love a string of unshelled peanuts too. You can easily thread these and hang them from a tree, or from a nail just outside the window, if you want to watch the little bird-acrobats closely. They will soon be quite friendly and tame.

The birds love an enamel bowl of water in the summer-time, not only for drinking but for bathing. When the weather is frosty, perhaps you could put out a saucer of warm water every now and again for the birds if there is no running water near you— many birds die of thirst in a district where ponds and puddles have frozen over, and there is no running water for them to go to.

Do you know the net bags that people take shopping with them? If you have an old one of those, fill it with nesting-material in the spring and leave it somewhere in your garden. The birds will come and peck it out through the holes and will fly off with it to their nests. You may easily watch them, and find great interest in doing so. Moss, leaves, feathers, wool, hay, hairs from your hair-brush—the birds like all these things, and will visit your bag until it is empty!

Nesting-boxes you may buy quite cheaply, and nail or hang on a tree branch.

Every garden has a robin or a pair of robins. The robins will perch near you when you work, singing a little, low, whispering song, eagerly watching for caterpillars or grubs. A robin is always easy to tame. You may perhaps be able to teach yours to take a piece of biscuit from your hand or even from your mouth. He will devour hundreds of harmful grubs for you.

Thrushes love a feast of snails or slugs. Many thrushes have their own anvil-stone—the stone on which they break the snail-shells in order to get at the soft body inside. You will always know the

thrush's anvil by the array of empty snail-shells scattered around it. Sometimes you may hear a click – click – click in your garden—it is probably a thrush banging an unfortunate snail on the anvil-stone! Go quietly and search—you will soon see the busy thrush banging away. At last the shell is broken in many places, and the thrush pecks out the snail's body.

Most birds feed their young ones on caterpillars and grubs. I have even seen the little robber sparrows pecking greenfly off my roses, ready to take them tò their nestlings. Swallows catch and eat hundreds and hundreds of flies a day. Titmice will often destroy the buds on trees, but usually they only attack a tree which has diseased buds. The tits do not eat the buds. They are looking for the insect that lies in the middle of the diseased bud.

Always welcome the birds to your garden, and make friends with them whenever you can.

Toads and Frogs

Do you like toads and frogs? Most people don't. I do, because they have been good friends to me in my garden, and also I think they have lovely, coppery eyes, especially toads. Look at one closely next time you have the chance. Do you know a toad from a frog? A frog has a smoother skin, and travels by means of startling hops. A toad has a more warty skin, and crawls very slowly. They like a feast of slugs, and if they find any woodlice they are delighted. They also eat things that are friendly to our garden, such as spiders (which eat such things as harmful flies, as you know), but as a general rule the food of which

they eat most is made up of creatures harmful to our garden. A toad in a greenhouse is a very good friend. I always keep one or two there, and they are most useful to me, besides being very tame. Did you know that a toad likes his back tickled with a straw? Try it and see! He will wriggle in delight and will put a paw behind to scratch himself in a very human sort of way!

Hedgehogs

These prickly creatures, which roll themselves into a tight ball when frightened, are true friends of the gardener. Hedgehogs eat vast numbers of insects, as well as snails and slugs. They hide in leafy undergrowth during the day, then come out at night to do their good work.

Earthworms

The worm may spoil our lawns by his casts of soil, but he is more of a friend than an enemy, so please spare him when digging your garden. He is a real little ploughman. He makes tunnels in the soil, which air it and drain it. He brings soil from deep down to the surface. He drags down leaves into his holes, which, in decaying, act as manure and enrich the earth beneath. He is one of our very best

172

garden friends (except, of course, where a smooth, level lawn is kept). You would be surprised to find how one or two worms can mix up the soil and move it. Would you like to see how they do it?

Get a glass jam-jar. Put into it a layer of ordinary brown soil. Then a layer of sand. Then a layer of sawdust. Then a layer of anything else you like— coloured beads, peat fibre, anything—and a layer of ordinary soil on the top again. Put in a couple of worms and leave them. Very soon you will find that you cannot see your nice straight layers—they are higgledy-piggledy, crooked and slanting, all merging one into another. Later still the whole of the contents of your jar will be so mingled together that it seems as if there never could have been any different layers at all! That will show you how the worm works in the soil!

Ladybirds

Ladybirds are very good friends to our garden; not so much the ladybirds themselves–those little red beetles, with their black spots—but the grubs that hatch from the eggs they lay.

The grey-black grubs with their short legs hatch out of eggs laid on stems that are already covered with growing and multiplying greenfly. The grubs go about among the fat and juicy greenfly and eat them up by the score, feasting all day long. Examine a stem or two of an infested

rose-bush and see if you can find the greyish grub of the ladybird. The ladybirds, too, attack and eat the greenfly, but not to such a great extent as the hungry and fierce grubs. So welcome the pretty ladybird to your garden, and let it do all the good it can for you.

The Violet Ground-Beetle

This beetle is useful to us in the garden because it loves to feast on caterpillars and grubs. Do you know it? It has violet edges to its wing covers. It cannot fly, but it can run very fast indeed. Its grub is useful to us too, for it lives underground and hunts for living food there.

The Green Tiger Beetle

This is a pretty beetle which you may often have seen rushing about in a warm, sunny place. It hunts and eats any smaller insect it can find.

Cock-Tail Beetles

These are the curious beetles that bend their tail end forward and upward. There is one kind you may have heard of called the devil's coach-horse. They are useful in the garden too, for they love to feed on smaller insects or on caterpillars of any size.

FRIENDS IN THE GARDEN

Hover-Flies

Have you ever seen a fly hovering in the air with outstretched wings? This is a hover-fly, and it, too, is useful in the garden.

Lace-Wing Fly

This pretty fly with its beautiful golden eyes has very fierce and hungry grubs, which eat enormously, feasting greedily on all the greenfly within reach. The eggs are rather curious, and you might wonder what they were if you found them.

They are laid on a leaf, each egg at the tip of a fine, upright thread. They are raised above the surface of the leaf in this manner so that they shall be out of reach of the greenfly that are feeding nearby. If you find these curious, stalked eggs, leave them safely where they are. You may be sure that the grubs that hatch out will do good work!

The Testacella Slug

This little slug is one of our garden friends. You may tell it by the fact that it has a little cap-like shell at the *hinder* end of its body, on the outside. This slug often goes underground to hunt for grubs. It will also eat earthworms, but it is more of a friend than an enemy.

Centipede

This is a long and flattened creature, rather like the millipede but with only one pair of legs to each body-segment. It hunts and eats harmful grubs.

Bees and Wasps

Bees are good friends to the garden because they take pollen from one flower to another, and this helps the flowers to make good seed.

Wasps, although they damage our fruit in the autumn, kill a vast number of grubs, flies, and caterpillars in the spring and summer, which they take to the nest to feed their own grubs.

There are many other insects, flies, butterflies, and moths, which help to pollinate flowers, but which also in the grub stage do damage to plants. These are half-enemy, half-friend, and we will give them the benefit of the doubt.

Now I hope you know all your garden friends and enemies and will be able to recognise them easily. It is a great pity to have to destroy life, but if we wish to preserve the things that are beautiful, such as a flower garden, or things that are useful, such as a vegetable bed or fruit orchard, then we must destroy the enemies that otherwise would destroy our handiwork. If we do it in the quickest and kindest way possible, we need not reproach ourselves for it.

CHAPTER XXV

THERE IS no month of the year when we can rest from our work and say, "Now I don't need to bother about the garden." You won't even *want* to say it, once you have begun your garden and take an interest in it. Even if there is no work you can actually do in the garden itself, there are always odd jobs to do such as planning what seeds to have, looking through catalogues, finishing off your own seed-collections, and preparing labels for next spring.

I will tell you shortly what you may do each month in your garden. I shall not be able to put everything in, because there is so much to say, but at any rate this chapter will serve as a guide to you for the first year or two. After that you will know a great deal yourself.

January is the time to read up garden books, and make your plans for the spring. Get all the catalogues you can and study them. Measure your garden and draw a little plan of it to scale. Now mark on it your idea for plants and annuals in the spring and summer, mostly keeping tall ones at the back and short ones at the front.

Your bulbs in bowls should be coming into flower. Keep them watered sufficiently, and stake very neatly with thin sticks any plants that need it.

Although plastic labels are quite handy, you can save your old ice lolly sticks for naming annuals or other plants. Wash them well. Dry them. Paint them over with white paint. Now they are ready for you to use in your own garden. You will find that you can easily write on them in pencil.

Look over your own seed collection to make sure the packets are dry.

Aconites and Christmas roses should be out in your garden. If you have a great many aconites, you could perhaps pot a few up and bring them indoors. They are very pretty in a small pot, and your parents would be very pleased with them.

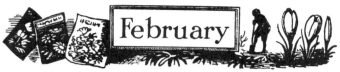

February

You must make out your seed-list and decide what annuals you are going to grow. Go and choose your seeds in the garden centre or shop as soon as they arrive. You cannot plant them yet, but it is nice to have them there, ready for the right day. Read the instructions carefully on the back of each packet.

Go outside to your garden and have a look at it. If you have not dug it over in the autumn, you must do so now. Look up the second chapter in the book and see how to dig properly.

Pull up any seedling weeds you see. They may begin to grow this month if it is mild.

Are your bulbs coming up in the garden? It is a good idea to loosen the earth round them with your handfork, very gently.

Look at your wallflowers if you have any in your garden. Are any of them loose in the ground? Firm them in well.

If you have a small greenhouse which you are allowed to use, you may sow the seeds of half-hardy annuals this month. Also you may sow the seeds of those perennials such as snapdragons, carnations, or violas which, if sown early enough, will flower the same year.

Crocuses will be coming out in your garden. Protect them by means of black cotton if you see the birds are harming them. Your primroses may have to be protected in the same way.

MARCH

This is a very busy month in the garden. Most of your annuals may be sown now, providing the weather is open and mild. Read the instructions on each packet before sowing. Some of your vegetable seeds may be sown now too. If you live in the north and the weather is very cold, wait until next month.

If you have roses, some of them may need to be pruned at the end of the month. You may also plant new roses this month.

If you have clumps of perennial plants in your garden, they will be sending out strong new shoots. If you have any wood ashes, you may spread these on your soil. The plants will take food from it as soon as it is absorbed into the soil.

Choose your outdoor chrysanthemums now and order them, or beg them from your parents or a friend. They may have some well rooted cuttings they can spare for you. You can plant them out in your garden this month, and they will flower gaily in the autumn.

A bulb (or, rather, corm) I have not mentioned before is the beautiful gladiolus. This flower blossoms all the way up a thick, tall stem, and there are many lovely colours. The time to plant your gladioli, if you have any, is now. Put them towards the back of the bed.

APRIL

Another very busy month! Finish sowing your annual and vegetable seeds. Finish pruning your roses. Watch for your earliest annuals to come up. Thin them out as soon as they can be handled. Water them if necessary.

Keep your garden well weeded now, especially in mild, wet weather, when the weeds will come up by the hundred. Keep your hoe going. Watch for slugs round your young plants. Put weathered ash, slug pellets or lime around any that need it.

Look to your half-hardy annuals and your seedling perennials in the greenhouse, if you have started some there. Are they ready to prick out into trays or pots? If so, begin to do this on a rainy day when you cannot do much work out of doors.

If you have violet plants, you may now divide them up and put them into your reserve bed or some shady corner, if you have one.

You may plant half-hardy annuals out of doors now, towards the end of the month, to flower in the autumn. You may also plant annual climbers, such as nasturtium or canary creeper, out of doors.

Look at your sweet peas. They have shot up, and are now good, sturdy seedlings. Give them little sticks to lean on. Then, later in the month, give them their proper pea-sticks, up which they may climb rapidly.

All your bulbs in bowls will now have died down. Some of them may have done so last month. You may now plant them out in the garden in some shady place, where they will flower for you year after year. You can save the fibre for another year, if you wish. Break it up well, and leave it out in the sunshine to air and dry.

You should have knotted all your daffodils down as soon as they became untidy with their long, straggling leaves. Pull them gently and see if the leaves come away. If they do, you may lift the bulbs and store them.

Be sure to hoe well and stir the soil about the roots of your plants. This will prevent the moisture in the soil from evaporating too quickly, and you will not have to water so much. Keep the weeds down with the hoe and with your hands.

Thin out your seedlings again if they need it.

Transplant those that will stand it to odd bare spots somewhere, so that they will fill them with colour in the summer.

Have you primroses, polyanthus, or double daisies? Take them up when they have finished flowering and divide each one into two or three clumps, each with a good root. Plant them in your reserve bed now, or in a shady spot, and they will grow into sturdy plants by the autumn, when you may replant them in your garden, having then three times as many plants as you started with!

Sow your seeds of biennials now, if you are going to try those. You may sow them in the open ground quite safely now.

Watch your roses for greenfly. May is a bad month for them, and if you get rid of the greenfly as soon as they appear, you will not have much trouble later.

Sow your scarlet-runner beans towards the end of the month.

Your garden should now be at its very best—a blaze of colour. The bulbs are over, except for a few late tulips. Your annuals are beginning to flower, and many of your perennial plants are brilliant with blossom too. Your climbers are high up your wall or fence, and your roses are coming into bloom. Now you see the results of much of your hard work and planning, and I am sure that you are delighted. It is fun to take visitors to see your garden. It is lovely to cut them bunches of flowers. It is grand to eat your own mustard and cress and to cut your first lettuce. No radishes will taste so nice as yours!

Plant out your dahlia roots at the beginning of the month. Remember to thin out the shoots so that only the sturdy ones are left on each plant.

Some of your plants are growing tall. You must stake them before the wind breaks them or bends them. Remember to give them their supports early, because then as they grow their leaves will cover up the supports in a very natural manner. If you allow a plant to break in the wind and then try to stake it, you will find that it looks ugly and unnatural.

June is often a dry month, so keep the hoe going well in your garden. Water, if necessary, in the evenings. Remember that a good soaking twice a week is better than a sprinkling every day.

Keep the weeds down this month, especially those such as bindweed, which loves to run up the stem of a plant and choke it. Hoe up the weeds while they are small. Do not allow them to grow big, or they will steal light and space from your plants.

Look at your plants every day and notice when any flowers are faded and over. Do not allow them to form seeds, but pick them off at once. You will remember that the main reason for this is that plants allowed to form seeds will soon die down and cease to flower. Also, faded flowers in your garden look draggled and untidy. (If you want to save seed for next year's plants, pick one or two healthy plants, and let them form seeds.)

If you want to pick flowers, do it in the early morning before the sun is high, or in the evening when it has set. Then they will last much longer in your vases.

Pluck your radishes before they are too big. You may take some sprigs of mint this month to the kitchen to cook with new potatoes.

If you have a flint or rock edging to your garden, turn up the stones and look at them every now and again, in case slugs have made their home there.

There will still be plenty of colour in your garden
this month. The tall hollyhocks will come out at the
back of your garden, and many of your annuals will
also be at their best. Keep the hoe going as usual,
and water when necessary. Remember to stake as
soon as it is needed. Pluck all dead blooms in the
garden, unless you are allowing them to form seeds
for a seed-collection.

If you are going to try sowing seeds of perennial
plants, such as delphinium or lupin, this is the
month to do so. You may safely sow them in the
open ground of your reserve bed as you did with
the biennials in May, providing you will remember
them, and will keep the bed well weeded. (If you
have no space for this, you may sow them in seed
trays, as described to you in Chapter XII.) Water
the ground well beforehand, or sow on a showery
day.

Look to the biennials you sowed in May, for they
should now be sturdy seedlings, and will want
thinning out. Keep the weeds down, and see that
the seedlings are not too dry.

Pull up your forget-me-nots now, and throw them
somewhere in a corner not likely to be used. There
they will seed for you, and you will find plenty of
plants for the autumn. Pull up your wallflowers
when they are over and throw them away.

You will find that some of your hardy annuals are now dying, and looking ugly. If you like, you can pull them up and put something else in their places—half-hardy annuals such as the pretty asters or perhaps a clump of perennials which will flower in the autumn. If you have any plants, such as chrysanthemums or phlox, in your reserve-bed, or can beg one or two from your parents, you will find these very useful in filling up bare spaces. Do not put plants that will grow very tall in front of short plants. Sometimes people forget that the small plant of phlox they are putting in will grow quite tall, and they plant it in the front where perhaps the candytuft was, and then are disappointed because it grows tall and hides smaller plants behind.

Remember that it is best when planting anything in midsummer to choose a cool day, or a rainy one. Plants hate to be moved on a hot day.

All the leaves of your tulip bulbs will now have died right down, and will be brown and dry. You can pull them off easily. If you wish, you can lift the bulbs now, and store them in a dry place. If you leave them in, be sure to mark the place with a label, or you will be digging them up.

You can take cuttings of your violas this month. Instructions for this are in Chapter XV. You may also take cuttings of such plants as pinks, carnations, sweet-Williams, and rosemary.

Put out a bowl of water near your garden this month and watch the birds come to bathe in it. They will love to come and splash there, and you may have to fill the bowl two or three times a day!

August is sometimes an awkward month in the garden. The flowers of early summer are now over, and the autumn ones have not yet begun to flower. Therefore our gardens may look a little dull and colourless.

There is not very much to do in August besides the ordinary jobs of hoeing, weeding, and watering. There are always dead flowers to remove, of course. You may perhaps be able to take seeds of some of your flowers now—those that came into bloom very early.

Are your rambler roses over now? They will be if you live in the south. Cut off all the flowering branches and take out any dead wood. Then tie in the new shoots neatly. These will flower for you next year.

Soon you will have to decide what bulbs to buy for your garden next spring. Catalogues will be sent out now, and you should go through all you can, looking at the pictures, studying the prices, and making up your mind what you will choose. One of the nicest things to do is to persuade your parents to give you a little wild piece of ground, or a piece of grass for your very own (that does not need to be cut at all, or at any rate not until the bulbs are completely over), and each year to buy some bulbs and plant them in your little patch. You may also plant your bowl-bulbs there when they have finished flowering indoors. It will be a real

188

beauty spot each spring, and you will be proud of it. Bulbs are among the loveliest of all things to grow.

Keep your garden neat and tidy in August, because, even if you have not many plants flowering in it, you can still give it a smart appearance. If you go away this month to the seaside, work carefully in your garden the day before. Weed it well. Cut down all plants that have flowered, such as sweet-Williams. Remove all dead blossoms and also *flowers* from other plants, such as violas, or delphiniums, because if you do this the plants will send out a new batch of buds, and the blooms will greet you when you come back from your holidays.

Finally, give all the plants a good soaking the day before you leave. If you can arrange with someone to come in and pick your sweet peas while you are away, it would be a good idea. As long as they are cut well, they will flower for you, and it is lovely to have sweet peas right into October.

September

This is the month of the pretty Michaelmas daisies. I hope you have some in your garden, and that they are well staked against the autumn winds. Your chrysanthemums are out, and, unlike so many other flowers, the blooms of these last for weeks! They are most useful flowers for the garden and for the house too.

You must plant your bulbs this month—all except the tulips, which had better be left till next month in case they push up too early and get their leaves frost-bitten. Remember to put snowdrops, aconites, scillas, and crocuses at the front, and daffodils, hyacinths, or bluebells behind. Choose good, firm bulbs, and refuse any that feel soft or pulpy.

You may also sow the seeds of sweet peas in seed trays or pots of soil, if you wish, as they will then make good little plants which you may plant out early next year in your garden. They will be more forward than spring-sown sweet peas, but they will be over sooner, of course. You may keep them out in the open till the end of October, and then it is best to move them to some sheltered place under a wall facing south, or into a frame.

You will be planting out your primroses, polyanthus, wallflowers, and forget-me-nots in October, so leave room for them.

·-OCTOBER-·

October is a busy month in the garden. It is a good month to *start* a garden, because it is a splendid time for digging and planning.

Dig over your garden well from top to bottom. If you have any well rotted manure, put it into the ground when you are digging. Manure stiffens a light soil, and lightens a heavy one, besides giving to the garden food for the plants. Be sure you do your digging well, so that pests are brought up to the surface, and the frost can get well into the earth to break it up for you.

You will find that if you have no manure you may obtain a very good substitute yourself by using well rotted compost from your compost heap or leaf mould made from old leaves. Sweep them up into a pile. Let them lie there till they decay. When they are old and rotten, take them to your garden and dig them into your ground. The plants will delight in the goodness left there by decaying leaves.

If you cannot dig your garden from top to bottom because it is too full of plants, you may simply spread the manure, compost or leaf mould around your plants without troubling to dig it in. The rain will wash the goodness down into the soil.

You may lift your Michaelmas daisies now, and divide the clumps. Other perennials, too, you may take up for dividing. Throw away the old, woody middle part and keep the young new pieces outside.

191

This is a good month to decide whether you want a new rose because November is just right for planting bare-rooted roses. Those who order their roses first are sure to get their first choice.

If you want to try taking cuttings of such woody plants as roses, lavender, and so on, you may begin now.

You should have finished all your bulb-planting by now—tulips as well.

Plant any primroses, forget-me-nots, wallflowers, etc., you have ready for your garden. They will flower early in the year for you.

If you want to try transplanting Christmas roses from another bit of the garden, you must do so now. Plant them where they will not be disturbed, in a place that is shady and has plenty of moisture. Container-grown Christmas roses can be planted at any time, as long as the soil is not frozen or water-logged, though they will settle in quickly if planted now.

You had better take up any gladioli you have and hang them up in a cool, airy place. They do not like being left in the frosty ground all winter.

Has the frost ruined your dahlia flowers yet? If so, cut them down, lift the tubers gently, and put them in a frost-proof place, covered up by an old sack.

Finish collecting any seeds you want.

NOVEMBER

Now, indeed, your garden looks bare! The frosts have nipped everything. Blackened leaves, hanging buds, leafless stalks—the garden looks a poor sight. It is difficult to believe that the same little patch was so beautiful in the summer.

As long as there is no hard frost it is safe to plant things in your garden. You can go on with your lifting and dividing if you still have some to do, but do not attempt any work of this kind if the frost is in the ground.

You must tidy up your garden as much as you can. Pull up all your own annuals by the roots and put them on the compost heap. Cut down all the perennials, but not too short, because if you leave them a few centimetres of stem, these will act as some protection during the winter. If you grow catmint, do not cut this back at all, untidy though it may look. The roots need a good deal of protection, and if you cut away the old greenery, the plants may die off in a cold winter.

If you live in the south, you can cut your chrysan-themums down to about 10 centimetres from the ground, but in a colder district you must not only allow them these stems but must heap fine earth over the plants to protect them from bitter frosts.

Plant any roses ordered by post now, providing there is no frost in the ground. Your roses will arrive neatly wrapped round with straw or sacking. If the weather is frosty, do not unwrap them, but put them in a shed until the weather is mild enough for you to dig the holes for them and plant them. Remember not to unwrap the roses until the holes are ready for them.

This is a good month to put up your bird-table. The birds will welcome it. Hang up a coconut for the tits and string some unshelled peanuts for them. They will be so pleased. The starlings will love a bone thrown on the ground. The more birds you can get to visit your garden, the freer you will be from garden pests in the spring and summer.

November is the month for bonfires. Keep one going in the garden if you are allowed to, and burn all rubbish.

Christmas roses should be showing their fat buds. Go and look for them from time to time. You will feel proud to take in three or four of the pretty flowers on Christmas Day. Look along the bed where your aconites grow, too. You may be able to see small round heads of yellow-green ready to uncurl on the surface of the soil. Your snowdrops may be showing green spikes too, and in a mild year even your crocuses will be putting up pointed shoots.

This month is a good one for finishing off your own seed-collection neatly. Make it as attractive as the show of seed packets in the garden centre! Put away the seed envelopes somewhere dry and cool.

Read any gardening book you can get hold of, or any nature book. You will be so busy in the spring-time that you may not have time to read or study much about flowers or gardening. So take the chance now when there is nothing much in the garden to do.

Some children like to keep a garden book or diary in which they put down each week what they have done in the garden. If you have one, you will find that the best kind is the book that has a page of drawing-paper on one side and writing-paper on the other. Then you can illustrate what you write.

If you do keep a garden diary of this sort, you will find that it is fun to colour the pictures or diagrams you have drawn. The book will be an excellent guide for you the following year, for by reading each entry a week ahead you will know exactly what sort of things will be likely to need your attention in the next few days.

CONCLUSION

AND NOW we have come to the end of the book, and I hope your garden has been a great success. Has it? What did it look like in the summer? How did your mustard and cress grow, and were your radishes hot and juicy?

If you are once a gardener you are always a gardener, and every year you will try more and more things and learn an enormous amount that you will never find in books. I wish you the best of luck and happiness with your garden, and that most important of all things to a gardener—the green thumb! Country folk say that if you have the green thumb, everything will grow for you—so I wish you the green thumb and the loveliest garden in the world!

INDEX

199

toads 171–2
Tobacco plant
(Nicotiana) 90, 92
Tomatoes 58–9
tools 8–11
dibber 10
Dutch hoe 8, 65
fork 8, 69
hand fork 9
hand line 9, 19, 56
hose 10
rake 8, 19
secateurs 10, 99, 134
spade 8, 69
trowel 9, 70, 116
watering can 20, 21, 47
wheelbarrow 9
transplanting 44–5,
183
Christmas rose 191
Lettuces 54–5
Wallflowers 63
trellis 34–5
Tulip 113–14, 116,
120, 142, 187

vegetable garden 52–3
vegetables, sowing 180,
181
Virginian stock 17, 20,
26, 62
Viola (Tufted pansy)
51, 75–6, 110, 136,
142, 179, 187
Violets 72, 181
Virginia creeper 41

Wallflowers 63, 142,
179, 186, 190, 191
wasps 176
watering 20, 21, 45,
46–8, 60, 68, 72, 124,
184, 186, 188, 189
weeds and weeding 46,
60, 63, 179, 181–2,
185–6, 188–9
window boxes 140–2
wireworm 164–5
woodlice 164

Zinnia 85, 90, 93–4

MY GARDENING NOTES

MY GARDENING NOTES

MY GARDENING NOTES

MY GARDENING NOTES